Hostel Hell

Robert Leslie

Copyright

Copyright © 2019 by Robert Leslie

The right of Robert Leslie to be identified as the author of this work has been asserted in accordance with the Copyright Designs and Patents Act 1988

All rights reserved. This book or any portion thereof may not be reproduced or used in any manner whatsoever without the express written permission of the publisher except for the use of brief quotations in a book review.

Printed in the United Kingdom   First Printing, 2019

ISBN: 9781690078630

'Everybody's vulnerable; see if you can tell me why you are more than vulnerable'

... said the Council lady. She went on to give me hints: 'drugs or alcohol, accidents, self-harm, domestic abuse, depression, suicide attempts?' Plenty to stimulate the old creativity.

'Yes as a matter of fact there are several things I haven't shared with you so far. I didn't want to, they are embarrassing'. 'Go on' said Miss Council, 'We are used to it here, nothing to be worried about'.

'Well I have had a number of accidents when I was feeling depressed from being verbally attacked by my ex, I could only take so much, then I hit the bottle and feeling that there was no point in it all went to jump off a bridge. I never got to it because I slipped on some steps, fell down and broke my arm'.

'That's really good' said Miss Council. 'Did this happen quite a lot?'

'Unfortunately this has been the pattern of much of my life, so yes, quite frequently'

'Thank you' she said, 'that's very useful'. 'I'm going to leave you for 20 minutes and go and put this to my manager. In the meantime if you think of anything else, write it down on this form'.

Sadly, without a history of drug offences, spells in rehab or prison time nothing of value came to mind, I'd just have to wait for the verdict being handed down. You can always appeal if they reject you; Citizens' Advice had given me the name of a legal firm versed in boosting applications like mine.

Nevertheless it was an anxious wait and I made mental preparation for 'No, I really tried my best for you, but you're not especially vulnerable, nothing doing'.

I had a come-back of sorts ready, 'Where am I going to stay tonight, all the hostels are full?' This based on my understanding that there is a statutory duty to house people in my situation. Later on she informed me, 'No the law's been changed, we don't have to do that now'.

Miss C returned, put a form in front of me and began reading out what it said. I was only half listening because rather than parse bureaucratese what I wanted to know was, 'Are you going to give me somewhere to stay?'

A minute into a list of requirements, restrictions and prohibitions, Miss C stopped, 'Oh sorry I should have told you that we are going to offer you a place'. The elation which suffused me was better than a limo ride with strippers and champagne. (I imagine).

'Come back in a couple of hours and we will have sorted out where you are going to be staying'. 'Yes, I'm getting a bit hungry; I'll go down the road to Greggs and get a sandwich'.

But I didn't, there's a pub opposite that ubiquitous snack emporium. The Shakespeare's scruffy exterior belies a rather tasteful inside. All the normal pecuniary caution of

the homeless blown to the four winds I ordered a pricey lunch and a pint of 'Landlord'
Joy, joy, joy.

It won't last, it never does, but believe me this social outcast was happy.

* * *

How I came to be homeless

Short version

I lost the place I was living in when it was sold and I had to leave. So I couch-surfed with friends for a couple of weeks in Manchester, Ross-on-Wye and Evesham. Then my daughter suggested that Bristol would suit me, so there I went.

It's gone down well enough with the various Council-related outfits here, so I'm sticking to it.

* * *

There's a far longer and more accurate version, which it has been convenient to ignore; I'll share it with you later.

Hostels, couches, floors
I slept in and on, September 2018 to April 2019

1. Lolli's Homestay, Dresden Neustadt, Germany
2. Kangaroo-Stop, Dresden Neustadt
3. Frankfurt DJH
4. Hostelworld, Hamburg
5. Kehl DJH, Germany,
6. Dover Castle, Southwark, UK
7. Edinburgh Backpackers
8. Joe's floor, Manchester
9. Manchester YHA
10. The Port House, Bristol
11. Rock 'n Bowl, Bristol
12. 007 Backpackers' Bedminster
13. The Backpackers' St. Stephens's street, Bristol
14. Wings, YMCA, Bristol
15. Central Backpackers' Birmingham
16. Tan-y-Fron, eco-community, Wales
17. River House, Cardiff
18. St. Christopher's, Bath
19. YHA Bristol
20. Dublin, backpackers
20. YHA St. Pancras
21. Hostel One, Prague
22. A&O Mestre, Venice
23. YMCA Bath
24. YHA Bath
25. All Hallows Rd, Easton

And at odd times in between,
+ Fiona's place, near Ross-on-Wye
+ Felix' place, Evesham
+ Charlie's place, Germany

The different types of hostel

Traditional, old-style Youth Hostels

Backpacker hostels

Council hostel accommodation

These three varieties of hostel differ.

Traditional, old-style Youth Hostels

Until recent decades Youth Hostel Association hostels had something of a co-op ethos, you were required to do your part by helping with some household chore such as sweeping the floor or cleaning windows. If you were travelling by car, it was prudent to park it out of sight and finish the last few hundred yards on foot. Car travel was for the effete, not hostellers, who were cyclists or hikers.

The YHA's website tells how they began:

> *The very first Youth Hostel was opened in Germany in 1909 by school teacher Richard Schirrmann. Twenty years later, following a trip to Germany, a small group of pioneers opened Britain's first Youth Hostel.*
>
> *The national organisation was established the following year and, by Easter 1931, 11 hostels were open.*
>
> *YHA is a child of the Great Depression. The welfare of Britain's growing urban population was a serious concern in the early 20th century.*

> *YHA's offer of affordable accommodation was an antidote to the poor air quality, cramped housing and harsh conditions of inner city life. It gave young working people an unprecedented opportunity to spend leisure time in fresh air and open countryside, on a scale only previously possible for the wealthy.'*

YHAs have changed and now copy the style of modern backpacker hostels. They are no longer cheap like they once were and the work participation is gone but now there are duvets not blankets, and rather amazingly, considering the original Spartan ethic, some of them even have a bar.

Backpacker hostels

The essential function is the same – providing somewhere cheap to sleep, but now there is emphasis on the guests enjoying themselves. This is achieved by offering the facilities that we expect nowadays - Wi-Fi, charging points, a bar, duvets not blankets and in some instances entertainment including parties and pub crawls.

Youth culture, relative affluence, gap-years, cheap air fares, Megabus and Interail contribute to demand for cheap accommodation. And if the price is attractive people are ready to tolerate a degree of discomfort - the Ryanair model.

Another distinction is that the word 'youth', the Y of YHA, no longer has much significance; with a few exceptions there are no age limits.

Freshly arrived in Bristol, without thinking too much about the issue, I stayed in backpacker hostels. I've done so much hostelling that I didn't really consider anything else. There's good and bad to them as I will be telling you.

One big advantage is that if they have space and you have the money, you're in. Try and rent an apartment or even a room in this crowded town and it's a different matter – you get inspected for suitability according to strict criteria; old, poor and jobless = undesirable.

Hostels aren't cheap though, a month's stay can cost the same or more than the same period in a rented room or apartment. This isn't a straight comparison either, since in a hostel you will be sharing your sleeping quarters with anything up to a dozen strangers.

What it comes down to is that for a 'backpacker', someone who is travelling on a vacation and wants a night or two in Paris, Berlin or Barcelona, the hostels you find within Hostelworld.com and other portals are convenient and considerably cheaper than staying in hotels. If you have limited money, staying in backpacker hostels means you can have a longer trip and see more places.

But there is another category of hosteller; people who don't have anywhere that they can call their own place. If you aren't an owner or living in conventional rented accommodation there's little choice beyond couch-surfing long term, living on the street or moving into backpacker hostels.

Such hostels are unsuitable for living in long-term. Nevertheless some homeless people end up in backpacker hostels to the extent that there are so-called backpacker hostels which are largely filled with long-term homeless people. Usually this is disliked by holiday travellers, since the two categories have little in common. If you read reviews on hostel websites you'll see negative comments regarding this.

In the past I have tried to describe modern backpacker hostels to (usually) older people who are familiar with only the early YHA type. I hope to convey what I like about the new incarnation, but as a spokesperson or lobbyist I usually fail. My description of the benefits and value for money failing to overcome the fear the mainstream burgher has of sleeping in a room with strangers.

You can imagine too that many women are particularly nervous when the company includes men as it does in 'mixed' dorms and/or bathrooms. It is an indicator of the degree to which norms change over time that for one slice of society both sexes sharing these rather intimate spaces is OK when three or four generations back it would have been unthinkable.

Council hostel accommodation

This form of accommodation has little in common with the previous types. You can't book it, online or otherwise, nor do you pay for it in the usual way either. It isn't intended for the general public; you need to be *vulnerable* – a term which has pivotal importance in the netherworld of homeless society.

Council documentation sometimes uses the term 'hostel' but you may see reference to 'Bed and Breakfast' accommodation. In my experience, only half of this is accurate, since you won't be offered a classic 'full English' in the morning. Bed + self catering would be more accurate.

* * *

That very Important V-word

Here's the actual council-ese on the subject:

Vulnerability

> *People with clear evidence of the following issues can be regarded as vulnerable. Please note that this list is not exhaustive: All referral agents should note that this guidance is to highlight that the categories list below can confer or suggest vulnerability. A clear common sense approach to vulnerability is recommended as is the need to be very clear with clients that they may have no support needs and therefore cannot be referred for services using the Housing Support Register.*

These are the allowable conditions

- Mental health problems; diagnosed or undiagnosed;
- Drug and alcohol problems;
- Physical or sensory disability;

- Learning disabilities;
- Long term diagnosed medical condition
- At risk of or victim of domestic violence/abuse;
- Teenage pregnancy
- Young people aged 16 or 17 years old. Also 18 year (+)former relevant child in care.
- A rough sleeper with support needs, whose rough sleeping history has been verified by the City's Outreach Service.
- History of prolific offending or at risk of prolific offending (includes offenders eligible under the previous Bristol Gateway programme).

Did you notice this part?

> *A clear common sense approach to vulnerability is recommended as is the need to be very clear with clients that they may have no support needs*

What's a 'clear common sense approach'? Or rather whose? Is your opinion 'clear common sense'? Or is mine?

This direction infers that decisions are made based on the ***opinions*** of Council staff; consequently outcomes will vary according to who is deciding. And it explains why I was urged to 'frame' myself as 'more than vulnerable'.

* * *

About the Council

Outside of 100 Temple Street there's a sign reading 'Customer Service Point' - if you aren't fluent in PolitiCorrectlish that means 'Office'.

Arrive before opening at 9:00 and you'll not be alone, especially on the first day after a weekend or a public holiday. Motley bods will be standing around. There may be a queue of sorts with a sprinkling of others for whom this British habit is unfamiliar.

Cigarettes are smoked, or more usually rollies are prepared as a way to pass time purposefully. Smouldering fags are held in readiness for a final drag and extinction. All are waiting for the-opening-of-the-doors. Within stands the man who will be performing this ceremony.

Our patience is rewarded, so now some adroit manoeuvring to avoid being queue-jumped. Done right there may only be half a dozen people ahead of you in the triage line. Next an ambulant staff person will come up and ask what your issue concerns, and for some categories, or if you already have an appointment, you will be directed or led to the deeper interior.

That area is more hospitable than you might be anticipating from the outside of the building which is sixties-ish design, featuring concrete panelling in medium-decrepit grey. By contrast the waiting-around zone inside has walls in attractive colours and the lighting is bright. I congratulate the designer on making pleasant a place people only come to because they have a problem.

There's comfortable seating, an island with toys for children who, from necessity, have been brought along, toilets and a couple of private spaces for confidential interview.

Not much distinguishes the Council workers from their clients; ethnics, dress, tatts, hairstyles, face ornamentation all shared without distinction, the way to tell which is which; the service suppliers usually have a laptop computer in their hands and an ID-on-lanyard hanging from their necks.

Remarkably, at least for he who has just spent a near decade in an isolated and conservative location, one staff member is a Somalian woman in full black costume. Perfectly appropriate one appreciates, since a considerable number of clients are from the same part of the globe, but a surprise nevertheless.

Judging by my own experience and what I have seen going on around me, it looks as though you will get the outcome you want about one time in three that you attend. On my first visit I was interviewed by a woman who seemed sympathetic towards me and my situation, she asked detailed questions and took a volume of notes. After a wait I was directed to see another female staff person. The vibe with her was utterly different; one minute of interchange and she delivered her verdict, 'Nothing doing, you aren't eligible'. That was a bit of a blow, particularly since first lady had me thinking my chances were good.

On another occasion, I was instructed to fill out an online application and sat down at a computer to do it. It didn't take long to reach part of the questionnaire, which seemed ambiguous, so I got up and sought help. The staff-man I asked explained how to proceed but his manner was ungracious.

Further into Council interaction I visited with a question about Housing Benefit – I had moved from one hostel to another and was paying more. You might think that this would not require much beyond a few clicks on a keyboard; you would be wrong.

No, it is not a simple matter, the process is this; client reports change; Council cancels benefits claim; client declares this an outrage; Council person stonewalls; client wanders off to find amenable Council bod; this latter says, 'Yes, strictly speaking what she said is right, but I'll sort it for you'. I said thank you and departed. Later, reprising the event to myself I may have employed a swearword or two,

It's not right though to lose sight of the overwhelming scale of the work that the Council has to do. There are hundreds of people applying for help every day; how do you deal with a problem like that? Clearly a system is needed and whenever there are rules, there will be people, cases, which don't fit exactly.

If you think about how life for vulnerables would be without our social welfare net, it's churlish to be disgruntled, although in truth I am not fully gruntled. My life is OK. It's been better at other times, but I realise that it could be far worse than it is. So thank you Welfare State, despite the frustrations in this land, we have it pretty good.

* * *

Here's where you are going

... 24 All Hallows Road' said Miss C. 'Someone will meet you there and this is the telephone number to call if need be. I probably won't see you again, so good luck'.

Next a bit of Googling to find the address; it wasn't in a part of Bristol that I know and apparently 3 buses would be needed with a walk of 0.3 and 0.6 miles at the respective ends. My knees and ankles hurt these days so I wasn't thrilled at that and set off hoping to find a better alternative. I did. Along came a bus heading in the right general direction, I jumped (not an exact verb) on and asked the middle-aged lady next to me the best way to my destination. It transpired that all I had to do was sit tight for half a dozen stops then walk a zig and a couple of zags through back streets.

My new 'hood looked to be a mix of trad Brit working class / immigrant with Council-esque notes; the street layout, signage, neglected green oases, all indicators of local government taste and not-maintenance. When I was growing up, a decade after the war, the word 'utility' was used to describe housing, furniture and other goods which were good enough for purpose but no more; cheap, no frills. What I was walking through was 'suburban utility' + litter + obese cars halfway across the pavements. This grot counterpointed once or twice per block by cared-for front yards with ferns, spring flowers and a surprising number of healthy palm trees.

Careful attention to Google Map's blue dot led me accurately to the hostel, a three-story, double-fronted house built, I'd guess, early in the last century. A concreted space out front featured what was left of a wall, a gate (missing) and two industrial waste bins full to the point that the lids wouldn't close. Every window of the house was obscured by coverings of motley sort.

A slim dark-skinned girl appeared and asked 'Did a black man just come out?' I indicated ignorance. 'I was supposed to meet him but my phone's on silent and I fell asleep'. All I could offer was a sympathetic smile.

The day was warm-ish, so I removed my jacket and leaned against the residual wall. Still another hour to wait for my reception and induction. I was assuming that a Council person would be coming, probably by car, to meet me here by the front door. Since I have lectured my scientist son about the degree to which assumptions can lead to error and disappointment (a view he does not accept) after ten more minutes wall time I tried the doorbell. Nothing, no indication that it worked or otherwise. Thinking 'there has to be a caf somewhere around here', I asked a passer-by which direction to try and he pointed down the road.

I still had with me my wheelie suitcase and a rucksack with a 10 kg and-a-bit load so this could only be a short recce. All Hallows Road runs parallel to a railway line which, fortunately, isn't very busy. The topography of Bristol and surrounds is hilly so railways have sizeable embankments, which is A GOOD THING. Such territory is unsuitable for parking or other exploitation by man, so nature can do what it wants any which way it likes. In this locale Big N has chosen to have a thicket of hawthorn bushes reaching for the sky, their white blossom emitting sweet perfume. My nose knew they were there before I saw them.

To the other side of the road is a school and you'd have to be wilfully blind not to notice it; the rails of the entrance gate are threaded through with a warp (maybe it's a weft, please let me know) of coloured ribbons. In front of this much yellow paint has been applied to road warning parent drivers to stay clear. Opposite there are metal posts keeping cars off another space - a person of imagination had a hand in this, since the bollards resemble stubby blue pencils with a red eraser rubber at their tips - a rather charming idea I have seen nowhere else.

Here the road turns and passes under a railway arch. In front is a playground centred in an unkempt grassy patch and with benches for parents, chilling locals and alcoholics. I walked on for a minute or so to try and get a glimpse of an important local feature, The Chelsea Inn. No could-be-anywhere backstreet dive this, rather it is a celebrated jazz pub one I knew of but had never voyaged out to because of difficult bus routes and times. But here it was now, on my metaphorical doorstep.

Now was not the moment for a session at the bar though, I needed to present as a suitable client when I met the hostel greeter, a slur of voice and a wobble of gait, not good. I may be an idiot, but I know that much.

As there were still 40 minutes to go before my appointment, rather than more wall-leaning, park bench time seemed preferable and although there was a touch of the bizarre about a bloke baggaged up as though just emerging from an airport now hanging by kids' swings and slides it was thus and it was good. Warm Spring sun making all the difference.

Opposite me were two men, the older one with Rasta headgear and a bottle. Snatches of their conversation drifted across to me but in a variety of English passing my understanding. Where I perched a man in perhaps his early thirties lay more horizontally than vertical. He was attending to his hydration from a can labelled in Polish. My arrival and presence puzzled him, he asked for explanation. I replied with a plain statement of facts. He voiced no understanding. His next words were to inform me what he was doing there, 'Impossible to work - today - not possible'. To one who knows the hopelessness of attempting constructive action while the brain is still dealing with chemical assault, his meaning was clear.

I thought I would show a degree of sympathy and solidarity by making a selection from the dozen or so words of Polish that I know. I ventured 'Piva nie ma'. My neighbour disputed this immediately saying, what I took to mean, 'No there is still some beer left in this can'. We sat in silence a while longer, he dragging the last from a cigarette stub. By now I reckoned if I did an old man shuffle slowly back up the hill I wouldn't have much longer to hover outside the hostel. So I said goodbye to the fellow with one word I was sure of 'Czesc', which does duty as both 'Hi' and 'Bye', as 'Ciao' does in Italian.

Even short, slow stepping didn't use up much of the remaining wait, so more wall-supporting followed, punctuated by the slim dark girl's next enquiry, 'Did he come back?'. I was still unable to confirm or deny.

My appointment time came and went. Before phoning the if-need-be number I waited an interval long enough to come across as perfectly reasonable, not demanding-aggressive - after all I am a social parasite. In my paradigm the appropriate protocol is 'submissive and grateful' - then I dialled.

'I'll send someone', said the voice at the other end. A few minutes later along came a pair of twenty-something ladies in a white van. I was greeted and led in.

It was a pleasant surprise to find that inside was considerably nicer than I expected. You'd have some idea of it if you have stayed in a mid-priced seaside B&B, say in Cleethorpes, Oban or Torquay.

'Come in to the office'. I came. This small room served for administration and the storage of cleaning gear, supplies, donated food, nine new toasters in boxes and diverse left-behind stuff. 'Have you seen my (insert as appropriate)?' was asked several times by bods who were at some stage of leaving.

'Leaving' is a keyword of significance; 24 All Hallows Road, is not intended as a place of permanent residence, it's a holding facility while the Council decides what to do with you.

Discussion later on with staff and occupants brought no clarity about how long I might be here or where I would be directed after. 'It could be a few days or a few weeks. I've been here four weeks', said one lady. 'But some of them get moved on the next day'.

What sort of behaviour you manifest has a lot to do with this. Despite the pleasant décor and furnishings you have to realise that the guests are not holidaymakers, as likely as not their last accommodation was provided by HM The Queen, functional and secure it would have been too.

Les Vulnerables (The residents) People are not shy about telling you that they've just been let out of jail, it's stated without reticence or shame. I found hearing talk free of the restraints felt at other layers of society very agreeable. Whether the topic is about dealing with the benefits system, crime or sex, plain talking is the currency. I like that.

A middle-aged female resident who would look just right as a library-staffer had just done three months for assault. Later she mentioned that her chances of getting a Council flat might be compromised by her record of arson.

Del By contrast, Derek, who refers to himself as 'Del', is a man you need little imagination to visualise making an offer which would be difficult to refuse. He is very black and very BIG, bigly big. Physical power oozes from him. But, and I sure hope it remains like this, he's all smiles and bonhomie - Lenny Henry and Big Frank Bruno combined.

Del wears comfortable clothing in a larger size. His body shape is full and round. Between where the tail of his T-shirt ends and where his shorts begin there is a generous gap filled with skin of bitter chocolate colour, cleft by a dark valley. He's unaware of this and hitches his pants up not very often. Mornings he appears in his sleeping attire, his shorts flapping open indiscreetly I alert him to this - 'Del, tiger's out of its cage'.

He likes a joke and pulled a stunt last night when he entered the lounge area lurching like a man sent to batten hatches in a force ten. I didn't know if he was ill or drunk, nor how to get out of the way if he fell in my direction. I'm not exactly fragile, but a couple of hundredweight muscle, fat and bone in my lap would not be good. Instead, Del reverted to normal mode in a flash, gave my arm a friendly punch, saying 'Gotcha' in his gravelly Cockney.

'Don't do that again Del, please', my response.

He took up position by the door to the back yard and began explaining those aspects of prison life you might only learn if you attend such an academy.

'There's geezers that want to stay in, 'specially in the winter. Know what I mean? You've got a bed, three meals a day and you can earn money – I was working as a chef. What's the point of coming out and being on the street? Know what I mean? The Council don't help you. What are you going to do?

They just go into Tesco grab a couple of bottles and dash out. Gets them 60 days and then they are back inside. They can't handle it outside, know what I mean? It's sad. You can get paid a lot if you bring drugs back, up your arse. There's blokes who organise it for you.'

Del continued with his back story, he done a lot of crime when he was young and bought a house with the proceeds, but not in his own name. His wife wanted him to put it in hers, but being sharper than yours truly Del could see what that might lead to. He put it in his son's name. 'Know what I mean?

'I do know what you mean', I told him.

He's only in his 50s but with a dicky heart. He says to me 'We're on our way out, got to be nice to people. I gave Old Bill a fake address so they didn't come round me mum's house and bother her.'

There's sadness in this funny man's voice. Maybe most older folk get this feeling, regret about things done and not done. The loop running on repeat in my head is an unfocused feeling that I have been a selfish bastard. As I told Mike, a good buddy, some years ago, 'If I wasn't a devout atheist, I'd make a lovely Catholic'.

One holiday in a bar in Alicante I met Ulf a gigantic Norwegian; there were a good two metres of him. These days an artist making videos satirising dictators and other unpleasant types, before he had been an enforcer for a drug gang and did some nasty things. Reformed now, recalling his past made him tearful. Some spectacle a massive man crying.

Harald, with whom I once shared an office, advised a way to deal with neurotic concern, 'Blame it on your parents'. He might be right but I can't quite manage it.

* * *

A man of about 35 joined us, deceptively fit-looking. By then we had got on to health problems. I mentioned that the doc had just told me that I have arthritis in knees and ankles. The 'fit' fellow said, 'I've got it in my hands' holding them up. 'Boxing done it; too much hitting people. I like sparring now. Not getting punched in the head'.

All present had 'issues' - the 'librarian' lady was subject to uncontrollable rages if she stopped taking her tablets. Del had survived a heart attack.

Now the slim dark girl came in and said the heating in her room wasn't working. She was cold. And to make her point, she undid her dressing gown to reveal a bony frame clad only in a thin slip. Del gave me a wink, 'I'd give her a sandwich' he said under his breath.

I may have been out of the country too long, or possibly it's local argot, but this 'I'd give her + *foodstuff*' is a primal sentiment expressed in a formulation new to me. I heard it again yesterday in The Cider House when a bird, a touch chubby but with long blonde hair - rating perhaps 6.5 on the Trump scale - walked outside for a smoke. A bloke near me informed his pal that he would like to offer the young dame an *ice cream* and the one next to him retorted, 'Get to the back of the queue'.

While on the subject of good / bad behaviour, something that lets down many 24 All Hallows residents is that they aren't fully house trained. The kitchen is a horror-show; used pans, mugs, dishes and cutlery abandoned where last employed or left soaking in murky, cold water.
This morning as I was about to make breakfast there was a pot on the stove, foaming to overflowing; rice apparently. I called to the probable owner who was stretched out on a sofa, 'Your stuff is boiling over'. He replied, 'Leave it. Let it take its course.' I couldn't watch this happen so moved the pan half off the burner and it subsided. I was a bit hesitant about doing this, since it is best to avoid provocations with peeps of unknown temper. But it passed off quietly, no blood or busted teeth.

So with a comfortable, quiet room to myself – carpeted, a double bed, heating, a window with curtains and no snorers you might think I'd be happy. You'd be right. I am, ecstatically. All those awful nights in dorms with every cubic metre crammed with other unfortunates now history.

Deep, deep gratitude, the very deepest.

* * *

The bad stuff

Of all the horrors you can encounter in the backpacker hostel existence, snoring is one of the most common and disturbing - what are you going to do about people like that? I don't know a good answer. Waking them up doesn't help, because you get a short remission then they are off again. Modest rhythmic snuffles can be tolerated and muffled with earplugs. But there are some varieties of nocturnal snorting for which smothering the perp by pillow would be favourite.

The worst ones I encountered in half a year and 24 hostels embellished the usual in and out sawing noise with added shrieks, groans and muttering. Fat, older blokes are the worst. Most of them are smokers I suspect. Women don't seem to do snoring, at least not the young ones. You get hardly any older women in backpacker hostels, so I don't know about them.

One time in Berlin the oriental bloke in the bunk above me was making such a racket that I took to kicking his bed from underneath and shouting, 'Shut the f*** up'. Two iterations of my treatment got him to leave the room and go walkabout for a couple of hours. But he came back and started again.

The next morning at reception I overheard a girl who had also been in our room asking how much a private room would cost - you know why. Unfortunately her idea wasn't viable since private rooms in hostels are inordinately expensive. The owners rationalise, 'if we can get 6, 10 or twelve payers in a space why would we make it cheap for a solo guest?' When the young lady heard the price she walked away disappointed.

Snorers are bad, but they are not the only source of disturbance; late returners from clubs; early morning leavers who make a racket zipping and unzipping their bags; über-bright LED torches and mobiles flashing in random direction, and whisperers. These ones mean well presumably but the hissy exchanges annoy as much as normal speech.

Then there's the low emotional intelligence types yacking interminably on their phones. One time after half an hour of this, I got out of bed and found a young woman sitting in the passage outside rabbiting on oblivious that she was disturbing several rooms of wannabe sleepers. 'Oh sorry', she said to my polite suggestion that she do this elsewhere.

Question: what is worse than sharing a dorm with a seriously bad snorer?

Answer: spending the night in close proximity to someone with Tourette's.

I hope you never experience it and that I never do again. Although the man I encountered looked normal-ish (piercings, tattoos being mainstream now, Gawd-help-us) and sounded so when I heard him talking to someone, he did a fair bit of giggling. When I'm reading something amusing I do too, but he didn't need a book in his hands. Fairly harmless you may think. Daytime I agree, but chortles in the night with the occasional fortissimo 'FUCK', not so nice.

People in this All Hallows transit camp for vulnerables know plenty about trouble in its many forms. When I mentioned the encounter with Tourette's-man, one lady said, 'My neighbour had that, it must be awful for him'. Another inmate revealed that she was a borderline case herself but tablets keep it under control 'Unless I forget to take them'. She had a tic, which made it appear that she was winking. Easy to imagine how that might bring about some awkward situations. Dr Will at the Boots GP surgery said, 'I feel really sorry for those people, they go through hell'.

* * *

Other bad stuff

This is probably as good a place as any to tell you what else is bad about hostel life (in a following section I will say what the compensations are). After the uncertainty of not getting a good night's sleep, for me the next big issue is that you usually cannot find anywhere quiet.

A noisy noise annoys. In the hostel existence usually there is no room where quiet is assured. You can be lucky for a while at certain hours of the day or night but those rare exceptions aside, be prepared to be exposed to one of the following: aural chewing gum coming out of the ceiling

24/7; karaoke and disco until 2 a.m. in the pub below; or a shoot up / car chase video on the telly. Those irritants are common to backpacker hostels; council accommodation features other and wilder nuisances.

The backpacker hostel, Rock 'n Bowl in central Bristol has a kitchen/dining area where you experience high volume un-quiet. It peaks when the Spanish residents are making preparation for a night of clubbing. At this stage, they've eaten, downed a quantity of vino and are feeling frisky. There will be music, shouting and most likely some good and less good–natured fighting; horseplay would be a better word.

One incident sticks in my mind: los españoles were arranged around the dining table when one of them grabs hold of another hombre and pulled his chair back so it was resting on two rear legs. Bloke-in-chair had difficulty in resisting this but attempted not to be laid flat on the floor.

The struggle lasted for barely half a minute and was greatly enjoyed by the principals and compañeros. No personal injury was caused, the only damage being to the chair; one leg detached in the heat of action. Not a problem; the original seat occupant simply placed this loose limb back more or less where it had come from then balanced the remainder of the seat on top - an amusing surprise thereby awaiting the next would-be sitter.

To get away from the surrounding racket so that I could think, I tried Bristol Central Library and the public computer room on the top floor is indeed peaceful but it's usually crowded and the plastic chairs are of a design which discourages anything beyond short sessions. By contrast in the spacious, largely empty, and characterful reading room, the ancient wooden chairs are comfortable. Why don't I go there? Because to get there takes at least half an hour and somewhat longer if the 506 bus decides to take a sick day. (It often does but there will be a valid reason, route obstructed by inconsiderate parking - so you mustn't take it out on the drivers.)

In any case, the library doesn't open until 10 am by which time half my daily ration of energy is already gone.

There's another factor deterring use of the reading room for computing – it has no electricity. To be fair, there is plenty of lively electron flow, to lights just no power outlets to plug into.

* * *

Bad stuff continued

The human odour – hunters stay downwind of prey they are stalking; we who get meat from a shop don't have that reason to be aware that humans are smelly. But stay in a multi-person dorm and the evidence is hard to ignore. This is why hostels block windows open - not a perfect solution if the weather's cold but at least the stink is diluted.

Deterring dubious dudes - When you are hostelling, keeping your belongings safe is another challenge. While the best hostels have multiple smart-key locks between the outside world and the dorms, some have nothing at all. In one extreme case, there was no reception person present throughout my four night stay. I never met staff of any type. An intruder could walk in to the building simply by close-following another legit guest. In that place there were no lockers and the only measure available was to keep items you really couldn't risk losing on you at all times.

Having said that, the fact that backpack hostellers are all in the same boat on this appears to have generated a measure of solidarity and respect for each other which is good, but there's no guarantee that all parties feel obliged to keep to this code of honour. I wouldn't leave my phone or computer unattended in a common room or dorm, some people do, though.

* * *

Night Music

One of the Bristol's biggest attractions is the highly active music scene. There's everything that you might want, whatever your taste. I like jazz and just last week at The Greenbank Pub I spent an evening at a concert by a quartet playing standards from the mid last century, my favourite era.

Even closer to my chambers is The Chelsea Inn. On Tuesday evenings a group performs who are known popularly as the 'Old man band' – this appellation is justified since the members are ancient apart from the bass player who is in his thirties. If you ever wanted to justify the expression that 'practice makes perfect', you could cite these highly competent musicians. They've only been practising their profession for 70 years or so.

Several of them play a multiple instruments; I've seen and heard the oldest party playing tenor sax, piano and a device which you could with a little ingenuity convert into a weapon of war. It's a construction in brass, a shade shorter than two metres, with a bore, perhaps I should say calibre, of about 15 cm. In the first instance I'd employ it as a mortar tube, but with a little work and a few more components I expect you could improvise a Howitzer.

For musical purposes, it serves to output the rhythmic underpinnings of New Orleans street jazz - usually the job of a tuba. But those wraparound oompah sounders can't descend to the basement notes of the Bass Sax, which you feel as much as hear.

* * *

Several, it might even be the majority, of All Hallows residents like music, popular music, and especially that which they know from their younger days. I enjoy some of it myself, but for me a little is better than a lot and I need to be in a receptive state and that's where there's a bit of a problem. By and large, 3 a.m. isn't when I'm in the mood for Abba or the Bee Gees. The man in room 6 inhabits a different time zone however; and he can't really enjoy his soundz unless the volume is full. I understand that, I like my jazz at concert level too, but at a different hour.

This music-lover is the same dude who came in through Ging's window back a week or so. He has difficulty with the drink, his dad was the same, he informs anyone within range.

One morning after he's stretched out on a bench in the back yard. His stream of consciousness is punctuated initially by groaning then after a while there are sounds of retching.

For this part of the performance he moves to the grass area to heave his guts out.

I'm just one open doorway distant when this begins and would prefer to be considerably further. Since I've clicked-keys enough to have a clear conscience about quantity of work done, I'm outta here.

Next day, there is much talk amongst the All Hallows membership about the same fellow's latest behaviour. In other circles, this would be couched in less direct language; here we call a spade a spade and a penis a cock.

The occupant of room 6 has been exposing himself. This is a bit of a first; we've had a fair range of unusual, and at times disturbing doings, but flashing not so far. One assumes that usually the exposée is a woman, and we have a selection here, Raha, the slender Somalian, Maria the Portuguese airport worker and another middle aged lady who has recently arrived. And indeed it is Maria who gets first peek. Surprisingly though, 19 years old Ging is next.

I'd share this errant fellow's name with you if I knew it; for now let's use Blackbeard, since the face fungus looks right for a Bristol pirate of long ago. When he next makes a public appearance, he collars anyone he can and puts the case for the defence. 'Didn't do it. Swear on the life of my children'. Some of those who are treated to this disagree, 'Yes you did you dirty fucker, Maria told me and I believe her'.

Maria, doesn't need to use much of her somewhat limited English vocab to confirm this to me, a simple hand gesture just below waist height suffices.

***

Morality

Swiss man and coffee pot

If I ask you to imagine a Swiss man, what image comes to mind? A banker - one of those 'Gnomes of Zurich'; a yodelling peasant in an alpine meadow; or perhaps a skilled artisan putting the finishing touches to a cuckoo clock? Then again, it might be a soldier with his standard issue pocket knife or an aproned dairyman boring holes in large rounds of cheese.

Stereotypes a-plenty, but none of them fitting the man across from me. This one a muscular thirty-something, dressed in jeans shorts and T-shirt was reclined on a sofa, boots on the coffee table. This posture his favourite regardless of who was sitting opposite and whether they enjoyed viewing the underside of his footwear. That was one indicator that he was a little short on couth, another being that his lengthy phone conversations were conducted at high volume as he strode a random path around this St. Steven's Street Backpackers' Hostel common room.

Many of his personal details were broadcast and available to anyone not using ear plugs. He is a trainer of something or other in the Health and Safety for oil rig workers field. The last engagement had been in Africa, now to obtain further certification he was booking a course for himself in Aberdeen. It was about escape from a downed and sinking helicopter and the price of the session a thousand or so for a couple of days. It was surprising that a man who could fork out sums of that order was staying in the seedy St. Steven's hostel, a place with a catalogue of deficiencies. The principal one in January being that there was virtually no heating. Everyone except this hardy Swiss was wearing outdoor clothing.

The kitchen was another of the problems; comfortably sized for say 6 people, it was used by perhaps ten times that number. Not all at once because they couldn't have fitted into the space, but at peak hours up to twenty would be in close-manoeuvres around each other. There were two sinks on an island with approximately one square metre of counter space and several appliance no longer worked as a result of careless or inept handling.

One evening Swissman is preparing his food, principally a large piece of meat. This he has on a chopping board and he is beating it with narrow edge of another board, hammer style. Whether to impress those present or perhaps following the kitchen rituals of his home country he was smashing the bejesus out of this slice of cow. The powerful crashes ensuring that he had his immediate surroundings entirely to himself, all others having withdrawn to a safe distance.

Cooking and eating done, he returned to the common room with its central twin opposed sofas and in-between coffee table. The latter he now employed for its intended use by placing a variety of cafetière device upon it. It was a type I knew of, but have never owned or used. Essentially it was a half litre stainless steel mug with a sliding sieve/filter to separate grounds from coffee liquor - a device intended for making coffee when a long ways from Starbucks. Swissman was clearly very fond of his apparatus. I asked him where he had got it. 'It was left behind by a South African, so I took it'.

These words were sufficient to give me the beginnings of a revenge idea. In my paradigm of behaviour, Swissman was guilty of sufficient offence to civilised etiquette to merit a measure of payback. And it was to be the loss of his shiny prized object.

I do admit that I had some reservation about this, but come on, Karma tells us that bad dudes will eventually get their comeuppance. So early one morning when I saw the coffee-maker in a pile of washed dishes, I removed it to the rear of a lower and out of the way cupboard. Swissman would be off soon to Aberdabber and sans cafetière. Ha-ha.

Now was that nice of me? Not really. Was it theft? Not yet, but it was going to be. At Christmas, I gave the apparatus a thorough clean, packed it carefully and mailed it to my daughter. She's outdoorsy and will appreciate it I expect. It wasn't right of me, but I've done worse.

*** * ***

Finders keepers

'Look what I found lying on the floor' said a fellow occupant of the Bristol YHA. He was showing us a ten pound note. 'What are you going to do with it?' asked a bod sitting nearby. 'Keep it, obviously', the reply.
'That's not really right', I offered. This did not impress the 10-quid-richer person. A second man joined in, 'It's not yours, take it to reception'. This too was ignored.

I added, from a position of somewhat arguable integrity, 'It's called theft-by-finding. It is a crime'. (I know from my own existence that in matters of this kind, your circumstances dictate what standard is appropriate - flat broke and needy, you see found money as a gift from heaven and it is.) Whatever level of hypocrisy my utterance contained, the money-finder was adamant. 'I'm keeping it'.

* * *

A floor in a pub

Years before in Munich I met a fellow who was equally free of qualm.

I had been sleeping for a while in the back room of the Winchester Arms - which we called 'The English Pub'. It wasn't intended for guest accommodation, just used for miscellaneous storage. During opening hours, access could be had from the bar, after that the only means of in- and e-gress was through a window leading on to a back yard.

A young Londoner was sharing the space with me, an interesting and somewhat scary fellow. In our chats he informed that he did opportunity theft when he got the chance. 'I gone into this building like I was a courier or something, I saw an empty room and a briefcase on the desk, I nicked it'. One evening he said, 'Have a look at this' and produced a short-barrelled revolver. I don't know where he got it nor what he was planning to do with it, but another acquaintance from those days had a related funding idea, 'You just go into a sub-post office with a shotgun. Easy.' Last time I heard of him though he was on the UK country fairs circuit, living in a van and selling helium filled balloons.

***

A shot rang out in the night

Guns intrigued me back then and in connection with a quite different adventure I bought what in German is called a 'Schreckpistole' which translates literally as, 'scare pistol', in English an approximate term is 'starting pistol'. These items were freely available in the sort of shop you find around the Bahnhof in major towns. The same quarter which has a high density of pool halls, money changers and joints selling immigrant fodder.

Intended for self-protection, these realistic-looking devices are constructed so that they cannot be used to fire a bullet, instead the cartridges you put in them either make a big bang - which certainly fulfils the 'scare' descriptor - or else they shoot tear gas. I bought one of the latter. Being keen to try it out, but aware that doing so in the middle of a city with plenty of Polizei was not ideal, I drove out to the countryside, lowered my car window and had a pop. Now that was a REALLY BAD IDEA - tear gas doesn't necessarily head out in a straight trajectory towards what you are pointing at; it billows in any direction it wants. In this instance a good deal of it blew back into my vehicle.

One thing I will vouch for is the effectiveness of the lachrymogenic vapour - I am willing to write a very positive testimonial regarding its quality. Tears poured down my face, and while needing to high-tail it out of my location a.s.a.p. in case my shot was drawing undesirable attention I had to balance that with the challenge of driving with no longer serviceable eyes.

Since you are reading this now, you can reasonably assume that I got away with this bit of nonsense.

Did you know that idiots enjoy saintly protection, not just by one holy bod, there's some competition for the role; choose from St. Gildas, St. Stranic and since 8 November 2016, St. Donald. You may want to inform yourself who to pray to if you share behaviour traits like mine.

* * *

Con tricks for beginners

You won't stoop to any of this, I'm sure. And so far, I can say hand on heart, I haven't either, but I find this sort of stuff entertaining – and I may need it for later in my life.

What I mean by that last phrase has to do with my *Retirement Safety-Net* . Living on £160 a week pension is OK, but you do have to cut back somewhat on the little luxuries. So what to do about this?

A man I now hate because he swindled me, bastard – I don't even like to recall his name – first got me thinking about this. We were talking about which European country gives the most generous welfare payments. 'T' had researched this and found that Luxembourg was best. For me that country would be easy with regard to language and lifestyle. I spent some years not that far distant in Strasbourg, France. However, Googling 'What's it like to live in Luxembourg?' brought up information which squashed the idea. Rents and other living costs are crazy high, so you are not actually any better off.

Most likely under the influence of the usual mind lubricant, the *R.S.N.* idea came to me. 'When I'm eighty I'll go to Sweden and pull a bank job'. I told 'T'.

The beauty of this is that it doesn't matter which way it goes; gettaloadadough and you can disappear on a long cruise or live an anonymous-but-comfortable life in a big city.

Alternatively, if you're nabbed they put you in a cushy IKEA-styled jail where you have a tastefully decorated room, Swedish meatballs *à volonté* and visits from the girlfriend at weekends. What's not to like?

But I'm getting ahead of myself; still seven more years before I implement that scheme. Back to my introductory course for con-artists:

Here's one I sort-of witnessed; I had made a very random trip out to Weston-Super-Mare, which name translates from whatever flavour of Romance language the original is in to Weston-on-Sea. I use the word 'random' advisedly since I had gone into the centre of Bristol on an errand and when completed, was without plan for what to do with the remainder of the day.

I have found that serendipity does a pretty good job in such circs so I went to the bus station and enabled by my bus pass, which permits me to travel free on any bus in England, I simply boarded the next one departing. No particular need to go to Weston; any trip out of the Brizzle metropolis was good enough reason.

It was a slow journey, calling in at the Airport on the way, and then on through farming country and the lengthy lead in to W-S-M. with much retardation caused by the many stops as we got closer to the town core.

Finally, about an hour and a half after leaving Bristol, we were there and I got off into very bright sunlight and the fresh sea air. By stages, passed in charity shops looking for book bargains I made my way to the beach and pier. From the look of the place, I doubt that much has changed since I was first there as a baby. Somewhere in an old album there is a picture of me, in bonnet with bucket and spade, on the very strand I was looking at.

Out of the breeze, the sun was making it a little too warm for comfort so I looked for a shady spot to take cool refreshment. Google told me to go back to pretty well where I had got off the bus.

The Dragon Inn, the local Wetherspoons was crowded but I found a stool at the bar and got started on the first of the day. Along a little ways from me two fellows arrived and ordered. The bar lady poured, the patrons paid and supped.

'What's this?' exclaimed one of them. 'It's Gold' (a cider) the bar person replied.

'I asked for Coors' said the customer.

'Sorry' came the reply and a glass of the desired brew was swiftly poured. 'Sorry about that', a further apology. This of course, as keen observers will have noted, leaves a very nearly complete pint of cider un-drunk and still sitting on the bar. The 'Spoons staffer enquired 'Do you want this?' and the customer said it would be a shame to pour it away.

Ten minutes later, all bevvies drunk, the two gents depart and I call over the bar lady. 'I saw them work that trick in another pub yesterday', I tell her. 'Good isn't it?'

It takes her a while to process this; she looks a little taken aback. Then I tell her, 'Just joking, they weren't trying to con you, but I have seen it done deliberately elsewhere'.

* * *

~~Bait~~ Eat and Switch

I don't know if the crims use that term but it suits, I'd say.

This is how it goes:

Man-one goes into busy restaurant orders a light snack and begins eating. His oppo comes in a little while later and sits on the other side of the same table, ignoring his partner. He orders an expensive meal. When it comes, the waiter puts down the bill (Americans this is the 'check') near his plate. Man-two eats his meal and when finished picks up the bill which relates to what Man-one has had. Man-two pays this small amount and departs.

Now Man-one picks up remaining bill, goes to cashier to pay. But the amount due doesn't match the cup of tea and sandwich that he has consumed and he points this out. The restaurant cashier accepts that a mistake has occurred somehow and takes the offered tea and sandwich fee. Man-two leaves.

Some way distant, or another day, the two meet again at different a restaurant, reverse roles and repeat. Neat swindle, eh?

* * *

A nasty incident

Do you know about the fight-or-flight reaction? It's a mechanism built into all of us which gives us the best chance of getting out of a nasty situation. Or it did through 99.99% of our history.

It works for physical threats, just the thing when a sabre-toothed tiger gave Ug the caveman a hungry look. But it's less suited for today's law suits and cyber-bullying, since they involve abstract dangers not the risk of becoming lunch for a big pussy cat.

The active ingredient in the fight-or-flight response is adrenaline, a chemical which when surging around your system sets you up for punching or running, according to which of the Fs strikes you as wisest.

I got a dose of adrenaline not long ago, unfortunately I was in bed, so the aforementioned F or F options were not readily available. This is what happened:

I've put off writing about this subject because it brings back memories which I would prefer erased, but nasty incidents were part of my hostel odyssey. This one was the worst: I'm in a four bunk room in the YHA and normally speaking this is a better-than-most quality of accommodation, for a dorm that is. I get to bed by about 11:30. I've deliberately left it that late because if you go to lie down earlier, you'll probably be disturbed by late arrivers. Tonight though, it looks as though I'm the last, everyone else is abed and quiet. I do my best not to make noise and use my torch instead of putting the main room light on. Golden Rule, I'm behaving the way that I hope others will.

Teeth brushed, stripped to T-shirt and shorts I'm in bed. Sleep takes me fast. Next thing I know, the room light is on and a big fellow is in the middle of the floor unzipping his bag and sorting through his stuff. Disturbing, unpleasant, unnecessary, avoidable - but there isn't a lot you can do about it, especially when you are sleepy. The zipping and un-z goes on for a long time - what seems like a long time. Perhaps if you stopwatched it it would only be six or seven minutes; enough to be irritating anyway. I've got my face covered by my hand to shield my eyes from the light, but it's only partially successful.

The guy is still mucking about, so the time comes when I've had enough and say to him, 'I hope you will be finished with this soon, I want to sleep'. He replies that he's 'only just arrived at the hostel', which doesn't really address the point that I'm making. Anyway I have indicated to him that he is disturbing me. Perhaps that will get him to expedite what he's up to so we can get back to the main business of the night - sleeping.

He clambers up the ladder to his bunk on the other side of the room from me. Although the room light is now off, he's put his bedside one on, that's also irritating, but I let it go. Some minutes pass, he switches that light off. So finally that's it, I hope. But no, now his phone plays loud rap music - why I don't know. Without any deliberation I let loose with, 'For fucks sake, you cunt', which Jeeves would also have advised to be 'Injudicious'.

The irritator jumped down from his upper level, crossed the room to where I lay and began screaming at me, 'Who you calling a cunt? Don't you call me a cunt. I'm going to make you regret that. I don't care who you are or what you are, you aren't calling me a cunt'.

I lay there, scared and with no idea what to do about this, which is rich since I have written a book with the title - 'How to handle angry people'. Here was a nice practical test, an angry man a couple of feet away from me, what does my book counsel?

I'd still say that the first three steps the book advises are generally appropriate, but in tonight's role play it would be best to apply number four, 'Avoid further provocation', that's what I had written and believe me, I was putting my words into inaction - I was urgently doing nothing to make matters worse. If he didn't punch me in the head and I just lay there, surely, I devoutly hoped, he would get tired of it and leave me alone.

A couple more angry words came from him but finally, doing nothing won the day, or rather, night.

Next morning I played dead until I was sure that he had gone, left the room. Then straight down to reception to tell them what had happened. 'I should have called the cops', I said. 'But I didn't because that would have ruined the night for everyone. Anyway I was tired and wanted to get back to sleep'.

The Australian reception guy did not express as much concern or sympathy as I would have liked but I told him

'I'm not sleeping in the same room as that bloke again'. That got me transferred to another floor so with luck I wouldn't have another unpleasant encounter.

I told Deborah - you'll meet her later in this story - about what had happened and it turned out that she knew the man. 'His name is Pete; he's something to do with the police'.

A month later, as she and I were walking from the YHA towards the town, we found ourselves closing on Pete, who was advancing from the opposite direction. In street clothes I didn't recognise him immediately but he had no such difficulty with me. I don't recall his exact words; but they were a rephrasing of what he had offered that night in the hostel. He had stored his anger intact; some people can; I have an ex-wife who shares the ability.

It could have all got nasty, fast. Fortunately Deborah intervened with an off-topic question or suggestion which distracted Pete. I used this interlude to increase the spatial separation between my antagonist and self - I definitely wanted to achieve greater than (his) arm-length. Deborah informed Pete that she couldn't stop and it brought the meeting to a close. She and I continued to our destination, a hotel a couple of hundred yards further on. Sitting in the lounge there we autopsied what had happened and I relaxed a bit. Not a whole bit, just a bit of a bit.

I hadn't met him yet, but Del would have handled this different, words would have sufficed, 'You're a good looking feller; let's keep it that way'. If you had ever seen him take a swing with his fists, you wouldn't argue.

I've just given you reason to think that I am a cowardly wimp. That's one way of looking at it, but my book on the subject of handling angries invites those facing the problem to think about what outcome they would most like, and in my case it was avoiding spending time in hospital. Seen like that I'm happy enough with how it worked out.

* * *

More aggression

Here in the All Hallows Sanctuary for Vulnerables we all get on pretty well together, daytimes that is. Nights are a different matter – and it's largely down to mood-altering substances. I can't provide a comprehensive listing of every chemical agent used within these walls; others here are experts. But none of us has much money, which means that if you want to get out – or is it off - your head, ethyl alcohol in its various manifestations is the natural favourite. That's not to say though, that there aren't pungent odours escaping from behind locked doors rather often. When the fire alarm goes off at two in the morning they are the most likely reason.

What the smelly stuff does to your outlook I don't know, I don't smoke, but I could write a substantial work on the result of alcohol in the bloodstream. The range of consequent behaviour includes all degrees of happi/sadness and from coma to violent rage. All of that can be seen here in the hostel.
And there is forever talk about how annoyances might be dealt with; Tony, known also as Cage Fighter - 'If he came in here again and had another go at me, I'd have to knock him out, there's no other alternative. He's a big bloke, a monster, but when they are that big they are slow, I'd punch

and get out of the way fast, there's no way he could catch up with me. Or I'd throw him over my shoulder, I do Ju-Jitsu, then get him in a neck lock until he's screaming for me to let go.'

Midnight Del is a tableau of growled wordage, unsteady footwork and potent lunges. That's about the time when I announce that I'm done for the night and am off to bed.

Recently he was describing his fix for the A.H. Sanctuary's problem with an intruding boyfriend. 'The geezer comes round to see her (the girlfriend) and she's been drinking so it kicks off. Then he has a go at Ginger (at 19 the youngest member of our band). We're going to knock 'im down wiv an uppercut then sit on 'im, call the police and say we caught a burglar. I'll get Ging to kick 'im in the 'ead, give 'im a black eye. Police can't say nothing, he shouldn't be on the premises, they got a report about 'im last time.'

* * *

Broken chair billy stick

If you were worried about who might call at your front door and wanted to be prepared in case you needed to cosh them, I can suggest something very suitable for the job. It's on display in the All Hallows common room. To be more accurate, there are four of them; the legs of a chair which has not been able to withstand the abuse residents mete out.

First the top rail showed signs of coming loose. Then one day it was off; next spotted in the back yard grass. Not a tragedy, if you place this chair against a wall, you can still sit on it and lean back. However if it's the chair doing the leaning not you, more stress is put on the leg joints than they can handle, so gaps appear.

Once again, this is not serious; you can hammer the joints back tight with your fist. When that's not sufficient, you can always take the chair out to the yard, orient it suitably and bang the jointed parts together with a brick. I had to show Chris the right way of doing this, he had the chair badly positioned so that a wallop with the brick was weakening the remaining parts.

One brick treatment is sufficient for one careful sitter, exceed that loading and the gaps open threatening to deposit the seated party parterre.

And so, one summer's day, there's a degraded structure which can no longer be termed a chair – if your definition requires that object-in-question can be sat upon. This is because the O-I-Q is now a triped.

The part which has separated is sitting on the table and looks mighty like something the early constabulary kept hidden within their trouser legs. (This is fact, not a smutty reference.) Known variously as truncheon, baton, (*vulgar Latin, basto- a stick helping walking*) *earlier, billy stick.*

You can buy a retractable telescopic security stick for £11.49 on eBay, but I think you're better off with a chair leg – one is ready for use now and three more are there as back up.
Now the reason I mention keeping a cosh by the front door is because Stuart a rather odd once-upon-a-time friend of mine does exactly this. He has a small shelf above the port of entry to his home, on it keeps a club. He's been angry

with me quite a few times, but never to the point that he had to call in Billy. I've been praying that the same degree of restraint will prevail in All Hallows, but I'm not confident.

One day I'm chucking garbage into the big container outside in the front yard and see familiar wooden elements. Another resident has been thinking along the same lines as me – 'Too dangerous to leave that thing lying around', he says to me.

* * *

From years of hostel stays, here are my suggestions for what makes for a good hostel:

A good hostel has

The really good hostels, those where it is evident that the owners understand which features are important for guests and provide them, reduce the negative factors as far possible.

So what makes for a great hostel? I'll list these according to Abraham Maslow's 'Hierarchy of Needs'; the fundamental necessities are shelter, safety, food.

Shelter

Hostels provide shelter by being open, (note that some hostels close for periods of the year), affordable and having the essential facilities. An important one of these is heating in cold months - this too should not be taken as a given. I had three spells in hostels where people wore outdoor clothing within the property because the heating was off and the windows had been deliberately blocked from closing completely. Complaining to the staff about lack of heating was useless because they responded, 'Yes we know but we can't do anything, it is the owner who has to. We have told him about it'.

In summer the reverse applies, you may find yourself in a building where the sun is beating in through the windows and there is no ventilation or air-con. If the dorm you occupy is a top floor or attic space you'll have a hot and sweaty night.

Security - for your person and your property.
The more barriers between the street and the dorms the lower the risk of unauthorised people entering the property and doing bad deeds. The approach I would adopt as a hostel owner or manager is 'belt and braces' so a guest must have either a key or know a door code to come in through the main entry and then as a second check pass in front of an alert receptionist before accessing the common areas.

To operate the elevator and/or to enter the floors where the dorms are situated you should need to use a key once more and then again to enter your room. Despite the inconvenience of so many locks, this gives you peace of mind knowing that it's unlikely an intruder can get to where you sleep and keep your bags and other gear.

Modern electronic key-cards minimise the nuisance and they have a further feature making them more secure than a conventional metal key - their validity is limited to the period of your stay, unlike a normal metal key, so the chance that a thief will have a duplicate is reduced.

For secure storage of your belongings the best answer is a robust locker or metal cage which you secure with your own padlock. It would be good if even jumbo 20 kg suitcases could be accommodated, the type that many travelling Asians have, but I have yet to come across storage spaces large enough.

A lockable space in the dorm is highly desirable; when there are no lockers or other secure storage people have no choice other than to leave their cases and bags on the floor or their beds trusting to luck and the honesty of strangers that nothing is spirited away. I have been lucky, nothing has was stolen in my 7 months of backpacker hostel life, but the worry that you might lose something important is always present. If my phone, computer or camera disappear, so do what they contain - contact info, journal, images and memories - their value far greater than the hardware.

Unfortunately many hostels don't have any in-room storage facility and when they do, it may not be up to the job. I've seen lockers which don't – because the fasteners are missing or broken and others where you can see that a thief could smash or remove the lock in moments with a simple tool.

Amazingly, wrenching locks from lockers is standard, perhaps even daily, practice at the Bristol YHA. A notice prohibits leaving items overnight in the basement storage area. So if a locker has a padlock in place late at night, presumably indicating that there are contents, a staff person will use a screwdriver to twist the lock shackle until it breaks. Then they haul out the cases and other items revealed and remove them to another basement room.

There must be logic of some kind justifying this; perhaps experience has shown that cases are parked by owners who use this area for longer term storage once they have checked out from the hostel, or perhaps they are just dumping stuff that they no longer want to travel with. Whichever; this will lead after a while to most lockers being unusable by current guests who want only a few hours of storage.

To my surprise, when my lock was smashed as described, on asking, the young female receptionist simply handed me another new one.

In addition, good hostels have CC TV cameras covering important areas. They provide a backup to other measures and a form of evidence when crime occurs. One time on a trip to Tel Aviv, a man who had been touring Israel by bicycle asked at hostel reception where was the best place to store his bike. He was directed to an area accessible from the street through a side entrance. He took his bike there and locked it up. After a short interval his bike was stolen.

Another door, leading to the street had been left open inadvertently and a thief took the opportunity to take the bike – how he defeated the padlock was a mystery. The culprit was clearly visible on CCTV footage which, if nothing more, gave the police something to go on and the victim proof of theft for an insurance claim.

Theft is not the only mechanism for loss. In cramped space, for example the bottom bunk of a triple-decker bed, you have barely enough room to turn over let alone sit up, so it is easy for small items to fall into the void below the mattress or slip down the side gap and vanish. Well-equipped hostels provide a shelf for such things as your phone or watch so they are easy to find when you need them. You are also less likely to forget them when leaving.

Safety

In third world countries it's not surprising when you come across unsafe electrics - I've taken showers in Central America under a so-called 'suicide shower' - the water heater above my head connected by exposed wires to the electrical supply. (These devices often give people a degree of electro-tingle, but I haven't read of anyone actually dying).

A report by the UK Institution of Engineering and Technology (IET) mentions,

> *'The wiring regulations have kept generations in the UK safe from fires and electrocution and no professional electrician here would work without them. Unfortunately, that message doesn't reach all corners of the world and some of the dangerous wiring examples our readers have found are truly terrifying.'*

You may encounter rudimentary electrical work in the Western Hemisphere too. In one particularly poor UK hostel a smashed electrical outlet with bare wires showing was inches away from my head as I slept. The electric hand dryers in the bathroom of that place had indications of amateur installation too.

Eating

It's great if there is a shop nearby open long hours where at least basic supplies can be had, but you don't always find this, three of the places I stayed in recently were at a considerable distance from their neighbouring towns and unless you had brought your own supplies with you, you'd pass a hungry night.

Assuming you do have the necessary to hand, now you need a place to prepare, cook and eat it. A top hostel will have a kitchen which is big enough and appropriately equipped for the numbers of people who are likely to want to use it. Don't count on this. You may find just a microwave and a random collection of cups, pots, plates and cutlery, viz a couple of dozen small spoons but no forks or knives, a sink with a tap which gives you either a torrent of near-boiling water or nothing and a half dozen frying pans but no vessels to cook pasta or veg in.

If there is a stove, the oven may be defective and a couple of hot plates don't work; for food preparation the only surface the dining tables. And all this while in competition with a crowd of other people wanting to use the space and gear.

Food storage is another thing which can be done well, but frequently isn't. The best is with boxes which fit into cupboards and fridges using available space efficiently. You are more likely to find plastic bags, unlabelled and stuffed into any free corner. This may be in a fridge, on a shelf or the floor and in a confused jumble caused by people raking through others' stuff searching for their own.

In my travels this year from 24 hostels I can think of only 8 which had adequate kitchens.

Beds

We haven't yet talked about bed comfort - to get a decent night's sleep requires not only the absence of antisocial people and/or snorers but more fundamentally a comfortable bed. This is something that is not to be relied on since there is no great incentive for hostels to supply anything beyond the cheapest.

You may find a sagging bed frame, or one with a metal bar mid-way along the bed and which sticks into your back. Then there is squeaking and rattling of the frame either when you or the bods above or below change position.

Mattresses can be thin foam through which you can feel the metal mesh support below. The good ones are natural materials thick enough to insulate you from this.

Duvets rather than blankets have become the norm, but sheets may be fitted and already installed, or as in YHAs, handed to you at check in for you to make your own bed with.

A strange oddity of A&O hostels is that reception will ask you if you want bedding. Who doesn't? Actually on two occasions I said that I didn't since you have to pay an extra for it. Once it was warm enough that I could sleep without covers and on another occasion, passing along a corridor I saw house-keeping's pile of sheets and pillow cases on a trolley, so I simply helped myself.

Nice upgrades to dorm beds are individual electrical outlets for charging phones and computers, a reading light and curtains to provide a degree of privacy and permit sleep when lights are on in the room.

If you are lucky, you will find individual beds rather than tiered bunk beds. The former are far more comfortable since you are not going to be subjected to shaking when the individual above or below you twists and turns in the night.

Socialising

A level higher in Maslow's model finds social needs; again there is much difference in how good and poor hostels cater to them.

It is good when there is a common room which is conducive to guests meeting others and talking with them. A cosy space with appropriate seating is ideal. I can think of one hostel which stands out as special in this regard, when I walked in it was like entering a party, I was immediately invited to sit down at a long table with others and offered a drink. The chat which followed was interesting, humorous and varied, the participants being from many countries.

In another hostel, the so-called 'chill out' room is a small attic room with decrepit furniture; it also serves as a dining area. It fulfils both functions badly. As a kitchen it fails since there is no sink or running water and to heat food only a microwave oven. As a lounge it is no better since the space is dominated by a TV. More often than not there will be a guest dozing in front of it while some rubbish action movie plays.

A good bar, with friendly staff and modest prices is a particularly valuable asset for a sociable hostel; they are rare though. And while it may be possible to get a drink, in YHA bars there will be high prices and probably no social interaction.

The German A&O chain combines reception and bar which often means that for either service is slow and liable to be interrupted. What's more that company chooses to have a large hall to house these two functions. Guests sit isolated in groupings of ones or twos along a back wall, so socialising is almost entirely absent.

* * *

Compensations for the bad stuff

Given the range of annoyances integral with hostel life, you may wonder what could make up for them. The answer is that in backpacker hostels, sharing dorms, lounges and kitchens puts you into close contact with people with whom you quite likely have common interests.

The sardines-in-tin proximity of dorms plus the birds-of-a-feather hostellers making for many interesting and fun encounters. There are young people in their early twenties who are already acquainted with most parts of Planet Earth, some with fascinating tales of adventure; other individuals with remarkable talents; and a sprinkling of rich people who slum it in hostels not because they are mean but because they like the freestyle existence.
For me, it's a paradigm shifted; hotels offer comfort - I have no problem with that, I enjoy being comfortable. But what is missing from The Dorchester to the Travelodge is

that apart from the reception, restaurant and bar staff, you don't meet and probably won't talk to anyone else. But in a decent hostel the chances are high that you will encounter people who have interesting lives and who will enjoy chatting to you and recounting their travels.

Here are some of the folks I have met

Shaun - a middle-aged man from South West England with accent to suit. At the time we were both residents of Wing, the rather poncy name for Bristol's YMCA. The building it occupies was formerly Bristol's central police station, the fine architecture has been re-purposed to make a superior hostel (not in all respects) - the most expensive one in town.

It took only a few conversations with Shaun for me to realise that I was in the presence of a man who is good at dealing with life's problems. He reminded me of Kevin M. (Another book needs to be written about him, should I live so long).

That Kev, when I asked him what to do in a tricky situation would typically begin his advice with an emphatic 'Easy'. Even if the matter was one which could lead to serious penalty, Kev had been there, got it sorted and laughed at his adversaries.

The media prefix the names of some prominent figures with the word 'Teflon'. Kev merited it too, his decades of activity not just in grey areas; some were just one shade short of black, and all unspoiled by penalty.

Shaun had similar ability in handing challenges. There had been early career hiccups; referring to YMCA's basement, once the police cells, he said, 'I spent a couple of weeks down there when I was young'. He'd made good though and the evidence for that was spectacular.

We were sat eating in the kitchen/common area, on the table lay a large book with a glossy cover, 'The world of Rolex'. I remarked to Shaun, 'I used to have one', as a reply he slid up his jacket sleeve revealing a premium example of that marque. The gold on his wrist wouldn't buy a house, but it would easily cover the price of a tasty car. Noticing my amazement, Shaun unfastened the strap - I should say bracelet - and handed me this icon of wealth.

The thing would have served quite nicely on a diver's weight belt. The heaviness such that you could hardly forget you were wearing it.

What was a man who could afford this symbol of status doing in a hostel, even if it was a good one? Shaun explained: he had sold his house, the greater part of the money was in his lawyer's client account and a slice of it gave him the funds for grey-market watch trading.

Shaun knows his way around Geneva and Dubai, places where shop windows glitter and price tags aren't needed . . . . if you have to ask, you can't afford.

There's a good living to be made if you know what you are doing, buying here, selling there. But you can't try this until you have established your bona fides with the merchants. To buy a watch at a price you can make a turn on, the shop has to accept you as a regular customer, one who isn't shy of five digit-prices. Shaun was on his way; he had recently upgraded his profile with a seller in the Swiss capital and had done some good business. He pulled up his other sleeve and showed me another prize item.

Whether at that moment there was another human on Planet Earth fitted out with a luxury watch on both arms I couldn't say but I'd imagine Shaun would be unique in the Western World.

This isn't The Dummies Guide to Grey Market Luxury Watch Trading, I can't supply instruction and in any case I would warn you against even making an attempt - too easy to get tricked and ripped off. Leave this kind of business to the select few, the people who REALLY know.

Although fascinated by what I had just seen and heard, I was impatient to get Shaun's advice on a less glamorous matter, how to go about bettering my situation - at that point a couple of months into the twilight world of No Fixed Address.

'It's easiest when you're just out of rehab, then they have to give you somewhere'. He told me. 'Trouble is they've just closed two of the centres, there's only one left'.

'What would I have to do to get into that one then?' I asked, not being a drug-user an obvious handicap. 'Tell them that your drinking is out of control'. That sounded reasonable, do-able. 'Where should I go?' 'The Compass Centre, Jamaica Street', he replied.
A couple of days later I went up there, to a back street in Stokes Croft - the cool part of town, (read: rather shitty -

graffiti much, garbage piles more, art - supposedly, pretentious - definitely).

I announced myself to the front door intercom and a friendly voice buzzed me in. A few quick questions at reception to triage me and then a wait until it was my turn. 'Would you like a tea or coffee?' another pleasant person asked. 'Thanks just had one'.

The scene around me impressed, this facility provides help to people whose lives have left the main highway. If you are hungry, have nowhere to sleep, are in the grip of an addiction or other sickness your chances improve when you come here. Dealing with such issues is what they do, every day.

* * *

The unknown runner

It's around midnight, I'm in bed in a dorm at the Bristol YHA and sleep is closing in on me. Then the door opens and after some torch work and positioning of belongings a person climbs up to the bunk above me.

I can't recall why we began talking but the content was memorable; this man is a runner and despite being momentarily off track he's making a circuit of Ireland. His girlfriend is accompanying him on the run and they are travelling light.

'When it's getting to the end of the day we look for a village or other habitation and ask people if they have a roof we can sleep under.' Pubs are good for this request naturally. It works; Ireland isn't their first tour, they have circum-run the UK mainland in a previous year.

I'd like to know more, but fall asleep. In the morning, he's already gone.

* * *

I haven't made it clear that the main compensation of hostel life that I have enthused about – the interesting people you meet (and the girls) applies mostly to backpacker hostels, not the Emergency Accommodation for Vulnerables type. That's not to say that the individuals in the All Hallows House of Crazies are without interest; they are, but of a different category.

To more or less extent they in need of help; some because of mental illness; others have difficulty managing their lives. Me, I had sort of given up on ever getting back to a regular life – my mental battery was flat.

But in backpacker hostels, the majority of guests are not there because they have an existential problem; they are mostly on vacation and living cheap so that they can do lots of travelling. In this crowd you encounter a wide variety of occupations, income and education levels and hear some extraordinary stories.

The Manchurian Brewer

The man of the title above has one of the most bizarre; he's a late twenties Englishman who has started a brewery in Manchuria. He tells me, 'The building I and my partner have is very cheap and we have a good market for our beer'.

He sells it at high prices to wealthy Chinese drinkers. 'A high price is the secret', he tells me. Expensive and British-made supplies kudos to the buyer.

'Lots of very rich people in China these days.'

'What kind of beer is it?' I ask.

'A dark stout, we call it Black Yak'.

I tell this young entrepreneur that I've been a hobby brewer for a long time and he says, 'Come on out to Manchuria and give us a hand'.

If my Bristol life blows up, I will.

* * *

The price of beer today!

You know what it's like with *cheap*, it's cool to get something for poquito dinero, but disappointing if the item fails to satisfy. Those one-pound sandwiches from the supermarket for example, not really enjoyable. (Nevertheless I ate three of them yesterday.)

Using the same cheap-but-not-enjoyable model Ryanair has become the most successful airline in history (whilst gaining a terrible reputation for customer satisfaction).

Wetherspoons pubs also practise the same 'bargain-price-but-disappointing' biz model.
What is a pub all about? Clearly they are places licensed to sell intoxicating liquor on the premises, that much we know

from the sign above the entrance. But I mean what is a pub really for, since any old supermarket, corner store or off-license will exchange alcoholic beverage for currency?

The distinction between drinking in a pub or while sitting on a park bench with a bottle in a paper bag is that in a decent pub there will likely be good craic.

Wossat? You ask.

The Irish Gaelic c-word encompasses the jolly banter and entertainment that you may enjoy in a pukka boozer. For those wondering how to pronounce the word, just imagine it's spelled 'crack', like the substance I hope you don't smoke.

And craic is the very thing missing in Tim Martin's Wetherspoons beer halls. His charitable establishments for the drinking man offer beers, good ones too, for as little as a couple of quid, which is a magnificent thing. But atmosphere? No, niet, nada, rien de tout, nix and oi vey.

Most irritating that.

Tim has my gratitude and respect (some reservations, when he talks and writes on matters unrelated to pubs, beer and drinking), unfortunately the layout of his places is unconducive to the craic, which this party considers equal in importance to the selection and price of the beer.

It's further evidence for my thesis that You Can't Have It All.
It's something that I am seeing in so many aspects of life these days - anybody telling you that you can is a charlatan.

So it is with some chagrin that I found myself becoming a prisoner of Wetherspoons. In theory I could have cut out the drinking, but some form of escape was necessary. (Yes, I know that is a rubbish excuse).

BREAKING NEWS BREAKING NEWS BREAKING NEWS BREAKING NEWS BREA

I have found the answer! Or rather it has been handed to me by my friend, debtor and chess nemesis, Keith – The Crown Tavern, a dive on Lawfords Gate, Bristol between Old Market and The Wild Goose – which is another place you will come across in my story.

Before adding my own comments, here is what **beerintheevening.com** has to say:

> *The Crown Tavern. A basic, no frills boozer just off the main Old Market strip, we initially thought that it was shut on approaching due to curtains drawn at the windows and virtually no light visible from outside. It consists of a single room bar with the counter at the back. Green seems to be very much the colour theme here and this included various paint shades on the wall as well as the seating and the curtains. Flooring is a mixture of old wooden boards at the front and some type of lino at the back. There were a couple of original*

looking fire-places with a tiled front and a dark, carved wood surround, although it did not look as if they were used. A darts board was off to one side with a couple of trophies on the shelf above and there was a small TV stuck up above the door showing some terrestrial television although at quite a low volume. There was a good crowd of punters in there on a recent Thursday evening visit, although most appeared to be of the older generation.

I attended yesterday, a Tuesday, and had the pleasant feeling that this could well become my local.

Before we get started talking about the establishment itself, the first point to mention is that there's a bus stop – for taking me home after a session – a mere rod, chain or perch distant. And that is a VERY GOOD THING.

(In Canada, years ago, we had a house on the top of a mountain and the only boozer in town was in the valley below. Man, I nearly died of hypothermia and exhaustion returning on foot in the small hours).

It is a very unoriginal comment to say that entering The Crown Tavern is like stepping back to another era. If there's a patron who has not had that thought, the explanation is that s/he's accompanied by a guide dog.

The place has those things which matter: a proper bar counter with a bit of a crowd around it. There are benches, tables and chairs in the remainder of the large, square room. No one-arm bandits pollute the area, nor is there even the faintest trace of yoof. There is no official minimum age requirement here; one exists by common agreement.

If and when there is music, it's from the glory days of the last century, when to be a successful singer the ability to sing was still necessary. On that note, (yes, I know) the Crown's several karaoke vocalists would get fair marks for a good try, less for pitch accuracy.

Enough of this descriptive fluff, what you want to know is how much is the beer.

The answer is £1.50 a pint.

Now I know that looks like a misprint, perhaps you're wondering if the decimal point should slide to the right by one increment. No I am giving you the straight gospel; one and a half quid. Of course to match the surroundings, it would be more appropriate to couch this sum in old money, pounds shillings and pence, but then again, it would look wrong; a pint for thirty bob. What?

When I began my public drinking career – White Hart, Hampton, Middx, 1963, the price for a pint of bitter was one and eight.

I'll translate that; one shilling and eight pence or converted to dismal guernsey, about 8 per cent of a modern pound.

As an aside, how much inflation does that represent? An average price today for the same glassful would be around

£3.50 to £4.00, let's say £3.75. Then (375 – 8.3) ÷ 8.3 × 100 = 4,418 per cent. Wow!

A fairer way to view price increases is by comparison to the prevailing wage levels. Mid last century, for unskilled work you might have been paid no more than £15 a week, Then your earnings would buy 180 pints.

Today, on minimum wage - say £300 a week, you can afford only eighty pints. Drinking has become a rich man's pastime unless you can find such places as The Crown Tavern, where, should you be so lucky as to still have a wage, it will get you two hundred pints.

By and large the C T patrons look well-nourished; I am not conspicuous. Dress code here is casual, casual – as distinct from the oxymoronic 'smart casual' insisted on by certain places of entertainment. No doubt about it, I and this pub are a comfortable match.

Now with a bargain glassful in hand I begin to integrate with the company. A fellow to my side is addressed by a man heading bar-wards. 'Anton, want a drink'.

'No, I am not drinking'

'A vodka?'

'Please.'

There's a hint of Eastern Europe in his voice. 'Where are you from Anton?' I ask. 'He replies with one word, 'Hungary' and I follow with 'No, just eaten, thanks'.

He's been here ten years; long enough to accept and tolerate that aberration in the British make up, the tendency to joke.

'I've been to Budapest a few times, it's a beautiful city' I tell him.

Anton agrees. I list the main attractions of this two-part city on the Danube; the attractive architecture of the parliament in Pest; the Castle on a hill in Buda. I also ask if he is familiar with the 'ruin bars'. These are an oddity I have encountered nowhere else. They are wrecked houses, bombed at some point in history perhaps, and now without any obvious concession to health and safety, have seating, alcohol and a vibrant late night atmosphere. Anton knows them.

He tells me more about his old homeland; it borders eight other countries has a long history of being in the way of invaders Mongols to Ottomans. This brings to mind a joke I've stored for a long long time.

During the last big set to, the Germans are marching towards Hungary and the Generals of that land are concerned, 'We are few, there are so many of them and we are such a small country. I am worried. Where will we bury them all?'

This raises a laugh.

Anton is clearly a regular; others chat with him and later, once a glass or two more has been emptied, conversation moves to how Hungary does better politics than we manage. I keep well out of this, don't want to cause upset on my first session.

I move to a bench under the high windows and marinate in the atmosphere. Truly this is a place in which relaxing comes easy. Just one thought intrudes on my agreeable reverie, I hear a nearby patron refer to this saloon as 'God's waiting room'.

Then I notice there's something wrong with my glass. I go and inform the octogenarian bar lady. She regards my empty, laughs and asks, 'Same again?'

* * *

Jolly Roger

At the top of my road, is the Jolly Roger pub, I don't know if the name is accurate, because while it's definite fact that the owner's name is Roger, his temperament I have not yet determined. But the Caribbean crowd he attracts is good natured, that may be a clue.

I went in there last Saturday – last watering hole on my way home, kinda thing. The patrons mostly ignored the one pink party in the room, several fist-bumped me in friendship. I must say I felt underdressed by comparison with others present, lots of sharply attired gentlemen and many brightly clad ladies.

* * *

Free beer

Have you ever seen a sign offering Free Beer? I have twice, and you might think, 'that's nice'- if you like the stuff. I can go one better than that though, from time to ditto I get a free pint, on occasion more than one, in places without the sign.

You'd expect there to be a catch when a pub offers such extreme incentive and you are right. The first time I came across the freebie offer was in Arizona. Under the headline was written, 'every day the sun doesn't shine'. As luck would have it, the sky was full of cloud, no sun. So I and my companion entered and applied for refreshment as per the terms posted.

'Day isn't over yet, fellers' from the barkeep squashed that idea flat. Grr.

The next time I thought the drink was à *l'oeuil* was on seeing a sticker on the wall of a bar, 'Free beer' and below that much smaller, 'tomorrow'.

Now to the even better method, one not available to all. Chance and genes have given me an appearance similar to Boris Johnson. During the period when he was seen as a humorous oddball, not the ambition-crazed politico of a few years later, on entry into a public house I was often met with 'Hello Boris'.

Depending on my mood, sometimes I would warble and hrmph a phrase or two of Johnston-speak, to entertain my audience. The probability was high that this would result in an offered pint. Merci beaucoup, Alexander Boris de Pfeffel.
Latterly, dressed in rags, (I exaggerate slightly, but the Jermyn Street, tailoring is a thing of the past for me now), the resemblance to BoJo is less obvious, and in any case, I

don't care for his political stance, even though his manner is still original and refreshing.

Something else seems to be working for me - and I hope you will accept that I do not exploit this deliberately - my homeless status. People have difficulty in believing that I am in the same social bracket as the bods in shop doorways. When they learn this they tend to be shocked and for the most part, very sympathetic. I'll repeat that I do not deliberately take advantage of this phenomenon.

One night when I was lodging in the St. Christopher's hostel, Bath, for lack of anything more appealing to do, I went to the Wetherspoons at the bottom of the town.

A couple of cheap pints into the evening, the place was very full - Fridays, you can't expect otherwise. I was having difficulty finding anywhere to sit, then I noticed a table for four with an empty seat and I asked the folks there for permission to perch. They're a couple in their late fifties at a guess, with a man about twenty years younger.

Now I've told you about my resemblance to a celebrity, well here I was sitting next to another Doppelgänger, only this one resembling the richest man in the world, (until Jeff Bezos of Amazon knocked him down a place). I'm referring to the founder of Microsoft, Mr. Bill Gates. The likeness was uncanny, the self-effacing manner similar too.

I began making a bit of nuisance of myself, by inviting the world's richest man to buy me a pint. As a joke I emphasize, to avoid you misunderstanding my motive.

He didn't appreciate my humour. The reason was reasonable, he hadn't heard of the celebrated Bill. Some people haven't, unlikely as that seems. Some people have never tried Coca Cola; I had a work colleague who said that to me once.

We reached the point that the son told me that I was irritating him. Fair do's, I might have been a touch annoying, so I shut up for a while. General chat ensued about why we were all there – cheap drink being a given. At some point I let slip that I was staying in a hostel and explained why. This had considerable effect; the son directly reversed his manner, and said that he was very sorry to hear this and 'Would I like another pint?'

As stated, I never purposely employ this gambit to obtain charity, honest, but it would have been churlish to refuse the man's generosity ☺.

Strangely, three months later Senor and Senora Gates were in The Long Bar, on Old Market, Bristol. It was odd to find them in that setting, which I think I can politely describe as 'rustic'. We were all pleased to see each other and reminisced about our Bath meeting.

'Bill' still didn't know anything more about the person I had taken him for. I told him it would be to his considerable advantage to work on acquiring the accent; there was a man a few years ago who enjoyed a complimentary stay in The Dorchester by checking in under the name Quentin Tarantino. No one doubted his identity, they didn't know what the genuine Q.T. looked like.

* * *

I'm a lucky bastard (if that word offends, please substitute, 'idiot'). Another free pint in Bath, two actually, came about by serendipity at its finest. On a dismal, drizzly, cold evening I was outside of the St. C and trying to come up with an idea for how to spend the evening. I wasn't aware of much choice, by contrast with Bristol, Bath is small and conservative.

Mid-ponder, a man asks me if I know where The Rifleman Volunteer is. I do, and rather than describe the complex lane routing, I said, 'I'll show you'. This fellow says that he used to know Bath a couple of decades ago and he's here for a short stay and looking up old haunts.

The pub isn't that far. When we got there, I began to say goodbye, but my guidee is having none of that, 'Come on in, I'll get you a pint'. I offer a polite amount of 'that's really not necessary' and then accept, as you do.

The volunteer is a proper pub; you won't mistake it for a wine bar or bistro. There's a surly owner on the punter's side of the bar, he greets me with an insult. The barman tells me, 'Just his way of being friendly' - and asks me and companion what we're drinking.

Glasses full, my new acquaintance is expansive about his life and work and it turns out that we have rather a lot in common. For a start, his business is in Chiswick, West London. I spent a decade in that area – although it has changed and I didn't recognise some of what he described to me. But his biz, or at least parts of it, are entirely familiar. I tell him that I spent a good chunk of my working life in sales which is the core of his professional activity. I have been through the ups and downs of that way of earning a living; we bond.

Beer now consumed, I'd be happy to move on – companion will hear nothing of this. (I realise that it's a bit cheap to duck out of buying the next round and feel rather shabby – but I am a homeless, surely that gives me some licence.) Companion unfazed, gets the next pints in quick – perhaps it's my outstanding company that he is really paying for. Next thought, he's not gay? I hope. No I don't think so, lots of talk about the girlfriend. But when the second pint is done, enough is enough. Good bloke though. If I can get this manuscript published, he's due a signed copy with a note of thanks.

***

Dear Martian, in answer to your question, 'What is people?' please see examples below.

***

Clarky, a nice guy

The man in front of me looked to be a street person - too thin, hair and beard which hadn't seen a barber in a long while, hoodie and trainer bottoms. 'See that thing, it's like a massage bench' he said indicating a long black object behind a jumbo commercial waste bin. 'You could clean it up and sell it'.

'I can't really do that', I told him, 'I'm homeless'.

'What's your name? I'm Clarky by the way,' I told him mine. 'Are you all right Robert?' I told him about that too. 'No, not really Clarky, I'm in a hostel and want to get a place from the Council, but it's not going very well'.

Clarky knows the system; he's been in the social care sector for years. He gave me useful advice and finished with this offer, 'If you can't find anywhere, here's my address, I've got a spare bed. You can stay for a night or two'.

Clarky went on to tell me about all the things he finds thrown out behind the stores in the shopping precinct.

'There was a pile of jeans, nothing wrong with them and a leather chair. I got an expensive coffee machine too.'

He takes them to his home, which is categorised as Temporary Accommodation - but less impermanent than mine which is Emergency Temp Accom. Some pieces he hoards, others he sells. It's a nice side line, twenty quid here, twice or thrice that there. To look at him you would never guess it, but Clarky is quite a shrewd and successful business man.

Two months later, I am wandering up the road from my new home out in Easton and coming the other way are two characters that I know; the younger one is Ging' (rhymes with 'binge') - who lives in the same place as me, the other is Clarky.

I never took up his offer of somewhere to kip if things got desperate, now it turns out that the address he gave me when we first met is just a dozen houses further down All Hallows, the road where I now live.

We exchange enthusiastic handshakes and greetings and Clarky invites me to come down to his for a cup of tea whenever I like.

And this I do a few days later although it wasn't simple; there are twenty bell pushes at the main door, none of them marked. I guess and press, then re-guess and re-press, with no response, then give up and go back up the road.

As the immortal Homer Simpson says, 'Try always comes before fail'.

The next attempt is in broad daylight and looking carefully - glasses on - at the metal plate with buttons, I see a very faint trace of numbers. They are in high-to-low order, not what I would have expected, so counting up from a just visible 17 I get to the right one to push for my friend.

A curtain is pulled back just feet from me and it is the hairy one himself. He opens the front door and welcomes me in.

'Cup of tea?' 'Yes, please Clarky'.

'Sit over here on the sofa, we're smoking and I wouldn't want you breathing in any of this'. The material in question is Skunk, an extra potent variety of cannabis. Ging' is there and another fellow who introduces himself in a friendly manner.

This chap announces that once he's finished his dooby, he's off to his missus. He's got a motorbike; it's just the thing for Bristol. Clarky shows me some of his new street finds.

'Wish I had more space, but then I'd only fill it all up'.

He's doing well at the filling, there's not much floor where carpet is still visible. He tours me 'round the rest of the flat. It's not bad, all the necessary - kitchen, bathroom, bedrooms one and two, even his own back yard. If Clarky was not a collector, I think the place could perhaps be made 'bijou'. As it stands, found objects everywhere, it's cramped, much. But he's not got to share it with anyone, so compared to my joint just up the road, it's a des-res.

Clarky says 'I grew up in prison'; what crimes took him there I don't know, to me he comes across as a really decent guy. It's a funny thing that, I have got to know a dozen or so ex-cons in the last weeks and to me they seem straightforward, likeable and for the most part intelligent.

I can't help thinking that our version of society is wrong in not making worthwhile use of such people.

* * *

Beggars belief

I had a pretty crazy idea some years ago; it could be employed in a variety of ways. A recent incident brings it to mind. I was between buses in the area they call The Centre, although it isn't that central - I'll let that pass for the moment. And the reference to 'between buses' is because I live on the eastern side of town but some of my activities take place in the southern sector – a journey which cannot be done on a single bus.

So I exit bus number one, hurry into Sainsbury's Extra (small supermarket) and look for a snack to keep me going through lunch hour because I will be busy then. Item selected and paid for I leave. Outside - and I really should have mentioned this before - are beggar.

It's a good spot for them, plenty of foot traffic, people standing around waiting for buses and what I suppose is seen in beggar perspective as the big one; there is a hole-in-the-wall cash machine or ATM.

The mendicants are careful about how they dispose and comport themselves, it's such a prominent location that police attention is inevitable. I haven't needed to try begging yet so I am unfamiliar with the rules. I'd think that any action which could be considered intimidating would get you into trouble and I've never seen any.

So when a beggar addresses you, it's mostly 'spare a little change, please' followed, whether or not some is given, by 'Have a nice day'.

As I leave store, I hear a standard beggar pitch and ignore it, but the speaker addresses me again louder, which is unusual. 'Do you want a sandwich mate?' he is asking me. This is most unusual. I turn back to face him and he fishes a packet out from under a grubby blanket, 'Someone gave it to me, I don't want it.' It's a triple pack, generously-filled, expensive sandwich.

I never buy them, too dear; I go for the not-that-thick cheese and onion ones for a single pound. They are alright.

Reasoning if that if I find anything dodgy about the packaging I will bin it, I accept the gift, thank the fellow and move off towards next bus stop and element of my journey. Waiting for a 75, 76, 90 or M1 I have time to inspect the item. Can't see anything wrong with it at all. I eat it later and since that was several weeks ago, it's probably safe to conclude that there was no contaminant.

Funny world where it's the beggars handing out food, I imagine Jesus would have approved.

* * *

Begging for fun and profit

I've wandered away from what I was planning to tell you, it's this:

A few years ago I was on holiday in Alicante, Costa Blanca, Spain and bored - out of season/cash/and my mind. Too hot to wander around outside, ergo justification for sitting in a pub and drinking my way through the afternoon. I settle into position on a bar stool and work up the necessary phraseology. 'Una pinta por favor, darling'.

I'll say this much for the Spaniards, they aren't too prissy about the conservation of their language. And the businesslike and moderately attractive barmaid proceeds to pour one for me.

I don't really care for pilsner type beers, and it makes no odds to me if they claim to be authentically Fracais, Deutsch or Mexicana. I'd far sooner have a drop of IPA, but *no importa*, beer is beer when you get right down to it. At least this stuff's cold and alcoholic.

Now as you'll know, once the first, urgent glug has been downed, it's customary to have a look over the surroundings and see if there's anything to keep the mind occupied. But there isn't as it happens. So I direct my attention to a fellow a little way along the bar. Fifty-ish, perhaps a little more; doesn't look like a native and for that matter not a tourist either. When he orders a drink, it's clear from the accent that he's a Brit like me.

'Where are you from mate?' I ask. He says 'Nottingham', and I reply that my granddad came from there. Building a bond you see – the soft skills course coming in handy once more. 'What are you up to here then? Is my next enquiry, and Tony, for that is his name, says, 'I've been in Alicante for six years. Came out here to retire, then my wife died one year later and I've been a beggar since.'

Shame about the missus naturally, but what I instantly want to hear more about is the begging. I've had a little thought tickling the back of my head for a long time about trying it myself sometime. It's the money-for-nothing plus messing with a middle class taboo that appeals to me. Course I am a fantasist.

'How's the begging going then Tony?' He tells me that it's not bad. There are quite a lot of benefits that you wouldn't expect.

'This lady, Maria, works in a bank. She stops by to see how I am and if I need something, she'll get it for me. I was sick for a while and she got me some medicine.'

'How much do you make in a day, Tony?'

He says it usually runs around 15 to 20 Euros. 'About what I'm living on from my pension', I reply.
'That's my pitch over there'. Tony points to a strip of park in the middle of the wide boulevard. 'I sit down next to the monument. You've always got to be lower than the people passing by. Psychology, see.'

'Where do you sleep?'

'Doorways', he says.

You wouldn't think so to look at him, the clothes aren't obviously filthy. 'You've got to be careful about your stuff though; thieves.

When I leave, I see that Tony's belongings are in a shopping cart, topped by a rolled up blanket and chained to a rainwater pipe outside the bar.

I tell Tony my thoughts on begging – executive style. 'You dress like someone who works in the city, go to a train station, Waterloo say, and approach people with this line:

'Sorry to trouble you, but I've left my wallet in the office and I've got no money for my train fare. Could you please lend me £4.50 to get a ticket to Twickenham?

'I think this has been tried on some TV scam show'.

Tony doesn't seem impressed. After all he is a professional and I'm a daydreamer.

One more beer, then it's time to move on. 'I'll drop by your pitch tomorrow Tony', I tell him. 'See you mate'. Next day, there's no one where he had indicated. That's pub conversations for you.

***

People who live in hostels

A broad sorting can be made; those who want to be in hostels and the unfortunates who are living *la vida hostela* out of necessity. In a brief stay, you probably won't meet enough people to get a clear fix on this; after a month or two it becomes obvious that few long-term residents are there because they really want to be, their reason is that they don't have, or at least can't see any alternative.

Crazies

A lot of the people who stay in Council hostels are a bit crazy. For the record I have no qualification to assess a bod's mental condition but I don't feel I need one. If there is bizarre behaviour and/or tales which push credulity too far I'm not going to be very PC about the labelling the exponent.

Richard

Let's start with him. We met in the Brizzle YHA. At the time I was still exploring wild alternatives to my continued lodging impermanence: yachts, shipping containers, vans, eco-communities, property guardian-ing, Buddhist and other religious retreats, and at the point that Richard enters the picture, a caravan.

Richard had the perfect looks for someone who wants to disappear; put him in a crowd of a dozen miscellaneous others and it would take someone with keen eyesight to separate him from background blur. As description, 'No distinguishing marks' would be entirely reasonable.

He told me that he lived in a caravan in Devon, but he wanted to re-join his estranged wife in Brazil. The only thing stopping him was lack of the fare. I asked him to describe the 'van and he did better than just with words; he drew me a sketch detailing the interior layout.

'How much would you want for it?' I asked.

'£500'.

'I couldn't go to that', I told him 'because I don't have it, but I could probably get £400 together'.

Such was the strength of my desire to escape the hostel life that I wasn't far from tying this deal down right away, sight unseen.

At this point P.G. Wodehouse's Jeeves would counsel

'Injudicious, sir'. Jeeves always knows, so I said, 'Give me the details of where it is and I'll go and have a look'.

But I didn't, some diversion came along and it wasn't until a couple of months later that I talked to the farmer in whose field the van was stored.

'Hello Colin, my name's Robert, I'm calling about the caravan belonging to Richard.'

In a short conversation, Colin informed me that most of what I had been told about the van and what it cost to keep it was far from accurate.

People can get things wrong without devious intent, that's what an innocent mistake is; I could give Richard the benefit of the doubt.

There is a further category of misinformation; you may be told a story which is sincerely believed by the teller but which nonetheless is untrue, made up not for dishonest motive but because in the teller's mind it fits their understanding of what's going on.

My unfortunate dad went in for this 'confabulation' in his final, demented years.

'That man on the roof has been there a long time' he said, looking at a house across the way from ours. '

Dad, that's a seagull', I told him.

Richard mentioned that he had a special dispensation which permitted him to draw Social Security money despite living abroad. I was surprised by this since believing that this was prohibited was exactly why I wasn't residing in Spain.

'How did you obtain that, Richard?', I asked.

'I did some work for MI5, they arranged it for me.'

I didn't enquire further; he wouldn't have been able to tell me - Official Secrets and all that.

***

Conspiracy Chris

A quiet man in his mid-thirties, Chris, on visual inspection, seems like quite a reasonable bloke. Mostly he stays in his room, evenings he emerges to make a mug of tea. Then he sits reading on the sofa or doing clicky things on a small device. He tells me that he has to finish an essay that he's writing. Ever curious, I ask him what it's about but he's not forthcoming.

After a week or so he becomes a bit more talkative and opens up on some of his pet topics. Details have faded since he told me, but the themes include;

'They're spraying the skies with aluminium compounds. Those trails you see in the sky that's where they've sprayed and you can see how the wind spreads the chemicals out covering everywhere';

and the insidious effects of 5G telephony.

'Why are they doing it Chris?'
'5G microwave radiation propagates better when the sky is conductive' was the answer.

I admitted to ignorance on this subject. Chris advised me to research on the internet,

'You'll find a lot of information'.

One evening, I'm in the popular-with-residents-hence-messy kitchen – there are two kitchens here, the second one gets far less use. Why? There's a research project for you; apply for a grant.

In kitchen-messy, there is a kettle, but not in kitchen-reasonably tidy. That's why I'm in the scruffy one; otherwise I try to stay clear. Chris enters and for once it's he who initiates a chat;

'I just got this',

he says showing me a small bottle containing a clear liquid.

'What is it?'

'It's energised water. Normally you'd put it through the magnetic field created by two opposing magnets – it rearranges the structure of the water molecule. But I've done it twice.'

'What effect does that have Chris?'

'It makes the water much softer and it gives it a lot more energy. Do you want to try some?' He pours out a bottle cap quantity and I taste it.

'What do you think?'

'Yes it's very smooth and there is a slight sweetness. Very nice. What does it cost?'

'I ordered it on-line from the scientist who developed it. I paid twelve pounds.'

I've explained to you that from the selection of bods I might sit and chat with in All Hallows House of Crazies, Chris is in the lead for intellectual compatibility. (Don't get me wrong about this; neither of us will be invited to prize day at the Royal Swedish Academy of Sciences.)

So I don't want to spoil a beautiful friendship by poo pooing his magic water. And in any case, what I know about re-arranged molecular structures can be expressed only in the manner used by schoolboys who didn't do their homework.

Teacher: 'Robert, tell the class what you know about rearranged molecular structure.'

Robert: 'The rearrangement of molecules structurally is an amazing phenomenon. It's a fascinating subject and it would take a long time to cover it in detail. Suffice to say that structures of rearranged molecules is a topic deserving considerable research.'

It's that or 'Dog ate my homework'.

So to satisfy those who want facts, here is what Big G has to offer on the subject of energised water.

Are effects of energized water real?

The following answer was supplied by Founder at True Energy Healing (spelling as found on his website)

> *Depends on what kind of energization is done to the water. I can say that the water I energize becomes full of energty that helps*

to calm down and soothe the body and mind. And it really helps .

The energized water is not a simple thing to do, because you need to make sure that the energies you put in the water are pure. Since water is so subtle, people need an extremely subtle touch when energizing water, to prevent the water from collecting energy filth from them. Most people that are performing healing arts do not posses neither subtlness nor purity of their energy ,so I would not reccomend anyone to drink what they have energized.

You can drink moon water in the same way. (When it is a full moon) Just , the moon water might keep you up at night so dose it accordingly. Drink sun water during the day and moon water during night.

That is the best thing you can do at your home, by yourself to get some of the energy benefits, unless you want a real expert healer to energize water for your therapy, at least occasionaly .

Enlightened Master N. True Energy Healing

* * *

I like to see some evidence before accepting an idea; but opinions differ about what qualifies as that. In this regard a certain Donald Trump has made matters harder. His denunciation of information which hitherto has been accepted as true has brought us to the point that any observation, irrespective of the probity of the reporter, can be dismissed as fake. If you are satisfied by supposition/allegation-without-evidence, your choice of 'truth' is now valid.

And here Robert launches into an area in which he has no credentials; skip this bit if you have a bus to catch.

What is truth? How about this? Truth is a belief which when employed leads to matters working the way that is hoped for / or as expected / or making a situation better. Truth is reliable.

Let's try a test: I believe that democracy makes people happier than demagogy. Is that true?

For an answer go to countries with autocratic government and also those countries which have democracy and ask the people in each about the system they live under, is it *leading to matters working the way they hope for, or expect / is their situation getting better?*

If there is a greater proportion of people who say 'Things are OK and getting better' than the reverse, then I consider my belief true.

It's not always simple that because there are many circumstances where one is forced to say, 'It depends'.

Salt is bad for you – yes it is if you consume too much of it. No it isn't - it is an essential requirement. Whether it kills you or keeps you healthy depends on the dosage; the level which is appropriate has been established by empirical research.

The problem with 'conspiracy' theories is that inducing people to accept ideas which have not been validated by testing leads to beliefs and actions which do not contribute to the general good.

I see that I'm losing the battle with my urge to rant. I will now shut up on this topic

* * *

For once I held myself back a bit and didn't make this point to Chris. The man is intelligent; misguided, I'd say, but not thick. And we did have a few other interests and experiences in common; there was no one else in All Hallows that I could say that about.

Chris had lived in a cave on Ibiza and another one at Grenada; I know both locations so I was interested to hear his experiences. He told me that he made his digs quite homely. The entrance required one to stoop but inside he had excavated enough so that there was standing height. He made a bed frame and a table and not too far off he dug a safe, a hole in which to hide valuables when he was absent.

One day in a blabla.com rideshare car from Valencia to Alicante we drove past a sandstone bluff, dotted with caves. They are a pretty good way to escape the summer heat. I'd have been happy to live in one.

There was a little overlap between Chris' arrival and Del's departure. Chris was not Del's sort of person and he teased him. A bit strange this since the big black man was friendly and considerate with others. I tried telling Del to cut it out. I did this cautiously; if you've already come across my description of Del and his early career, you'll understand why.

'New Age Traveller' is the term Del used for Chris and when one day Chris appeared clad in those emblematic baggy crutch pants favoured by that ilk, I had to concede, N.A.T. was about right.

One day Chris was struggling to open a tin can and this was the first time that I grasped that he was rather seriously disabled. His left arm and hand are not much good for anything; he can't grip or apply any force. The best he can do is to rest items on his arm the way waiters do with plates if they have many to carry.

'What happened to you?'

Chris told me matter-of-factly. 'I tried to kill myself, I cut my arm with a knife, removed the muscle and tendons'.

Now a hospital is attempting to reconstruct the limb. It's going to take a long time and it will be painful.

I beat myself up for my own idiocies, but by heaven (there is no such place, but the word sounds nice) I've got off lightly.

* * *

Kev

He's the general factotum in the 007 - Bristol's most awful (backpacker) hostel. Kevin likes fast food, playing rugby and admiration; a bit of fighting's OK too. That's brought a certain amount of inconvenience - he's ankle-tagged and subject to a seven am to seven pm curfew for 60 days - but 'I got the internet put in - I can watch videos'.

Kev explains the unfairness of his situation, 'This parking warden was putting going to put a ticket on the car and I told him to hold on. I didn't hit him; he says I did, so they done me for swearing and common assault. They done me for it before, that's why I'm curfewed now'.

He's not got a boxer's build, too much ballast around the middle, but you wouldn't want him giving you a tickle either.

He's done his knees in but that don't stop him playing rugby. 'Are you going to come down to the match?'

'I'd like to Kev, but I play chess on Saturdays'.

'Come down to the club after and have a drink. Tell them you're a friend of mine, they will let you in'.

Luckily the giant Argentinean, a long-term 007 resident, is a keen fan of the game and he gladly accepts Kev's invitation. Rodrigo's dimensions are off the scale found on human-measuring equipment; his head doesn't graze the ceiling, but he has to be careful with doorways. I doubt if he has any interest in weighing himself either, he would leave a trail of damaged machines. For all this he is a man of mild manner and keeps himself to himself but talk of rugby brings this big bear out of hibernation. 'Si, I come to game'. Kev is very happy about this.

My day takes its course and I don't see Kev again but I encounter some of the other long-term inmates; they tell me 'Kev scored a try; he's very pleased with himself'.

The following morning, Kev is there with bucket and mop - his main work tools and he asks, 'Were they talking about me?' I know a request for ego-stroking when I hear one, so I reply, 'They certainly were Kev, you impressed everybody'.

Kev glows with satisfaction and I think I have gained a point or two of favour with him. This might come in useful since the 007 operates on principles the Mafia would approve; with-us or against-us, forget reasonable compromise. When fault or injury is perceived, matters are settled their way.

I was kidding myself though; it turns out a couple of weeks later that obsequious flattery buys no concession.

* * *

Dave of the Long Bar

A tall bloke, quite snappily dressed for an old un, discussing the war – it's only 80 years ago – with a mate. Another fellow voices his contrary opinion and Dave is dismissive. When this party leaves a little later, Dave voices an unflattering opinion of him.

I'm sitting on a bar stool adjacent to all this and mention that I know something of what went on in Germany back then since I have spent rather a lot of time in that country. The conversation moves to more general topics then veers off at a tangent.

Dave has something up his literal sleeve, and it's very shiny and very expensive. I catch just a glimpse but I think I know what it is, 'Is that a Rolex you've got?'

Dave lets a bit more wrist protrude and the answer is sparkling in front of me. This is not a rubbish Chinky knock-off, it's the real deal. I tell Dave,

'That's a GMT Master isn't it? I used have one. Mine had the black bezel'.

(That's the ring with numbers on it which supposedly can be used for measuring speed. But really, it's just another gadgety feature for man-boys to show off with.)

Or so I am able to think now, a couple of decades ago I would never have said that, since this model of watch is hugely James Bond emblematic.

I enquire what they cost these days – mine, long ago and second-hand set me back £300 Later I look this up on the web; they're a bit dearer now, £7,150 for the basic stainless steel model. You can have a little embellishment in gold, for just three grand more.

However Dave says, 'I didn't pay for it. I got it from a jewellers, but I didn't pay for it'. Intriguing!

I must have indicated with some aspect of body language that I would like to know more. Dave delivers without reticence. 'I'm a con man'.

Then the big one: 'Everyone in this pub is a criminal'.

He knows them all, he says. He grew up with them. If he's right, I'd completely misread this mid-afternoon crowd of patrons. I had them as close-to-expiry, harmless old duffers.

Shows how wrong you can be.

* * *

Caroline

I've mentioned her before, but now a bit more tittle-tattle has come my way and it sheds additional light. Dee tells me,

'She's gone now'.

I reply,

'I wanted to say goodbye to her. She seemed a bit simple, not really able to take care of herself, but good natured'.

Dee puts me right on that, 'No, she's a working girl, I seen her up the road, soliciting'.

There's more.

'When she left, she crept out early in the morning. She didn't want anyone to catch her; she owed them all money'.

Well that makes me wrong X 2 as judge of character.

* * *

Fat Kevin

A large man busy on his laptop in the drinks-'n-dining area of the Bristol YHA. Unexceptional, quotidian you think. What with booking the next flight / bus / place to stay / blogging / transacting transactions / maintaining contact with friends and family, keyboards in hostels are busy and fingers active.

What this character was doing was booking a month long cruise around South America and negotiating a bargain price. Cheap cruising is one of his two specialities. The other, equally intriguing for me, is online currency trading, which is what pays for the boaty living.

The secret to getting an unusually low price on a cruise liner is to wait until the last moment. There is no point in a ship sailing with unoccupied cabins, since the ticket price is only one of the revenue sources that a passenger represents. Further money is made by selling alcohol, items from the gift shop, tours around the places where the ship stops and probably more things I know nothing of, never having been on a cruise so far.

For the above reasons, in the final few days, it's a buyer's market. If the shipping line wants two thousand pounds, you offer half that and say, 'There are other cruises I'm looking at', in effect, 'take it or leave it'.

Following this pattern, Kevin had negotiated his month in the Southern Hemisphere for £1,400, which at an average of just over forty pounds a day was no more expensive than hanging around in Bristol.

That was the pattern of his life, cruise-hostel-cruise-hostel-cruise-hostel occasionally broken by visits to his mum in South Africa, son in Australia and sundry other bods in Rhodesia – as he would prefer to call it, since that's where he grew up – Zimbabwe to those who follow the news.

Strangely for one whose life is organised primarily on screen, big K wasn't very computer-able. Since the second activity he was expert in was speculating in the small value differences between the Ozzie dollar, the US version and the South African Rand, you'd think he'd be a wiz at simple personal banking stuff. But he wasn't.

He wanted to move some money from his account to his mum's and following multiple failed attempts asked me if I could help. I tried, thinking that my good deed in sorting this for him would generate a degree of indebtedness. This, in the hope that he might share with me the secrets of currency trading.

After half an hour I gave up. To do what he wanted required a program which wasn't on his computer and although I manage to install one, it didn't work. So my efforts achieved nothing more than his had. So much for obtaining leverage.

Despite the lack of computer mastery, Kev was earning sixty pounds per day, he said. That's per trading day, which is not seven in a week, but five – and also minus holidays. This was just enough to pay for his lifestyle.

I'd like to have that level of income for the few hours that the trading process takes but I've read around the topic and it appears that almost everybody who tries it loses their shirt.

I put this point to Kevin and he says, 'I put in buying orders and stops, once they are set up, I know precisely how much I will earn or lose'.

Later he informs that his working capital is AUS $160,000. With this sum, tiny percentage differences in exchange rates can generate profits of the order he had said. This rules me out – although there was a time when . . . (that's for another book).

Kev's busy, stuff to organise. He gets up and goes. And that's that, probably won't see him again.

But I do, three months later. I am flip-flopping residence between Bristol and Bath, the spring season prices for hostels are creeping up and although it is a very touristy place Bath accommodation is somehow cheaper than Bristol's.

During the week I am often in either the Rock 'n Bowl in central Bristol or the YHA, come the weekend, mostly I'm back in Bath at the St. Christopher. But this weekend, the St C is full. I'm not upset by this because I don't really like the place. Yes it's cheap and there is a free-but-basic breakfast. The big drawback is the nightly thump, thump, thump music until 2 am; the bar/restaurant transforms into a disco. There are other things about the place I don't like, as you'll see elsewhere in this account.

* * *

Bath YHA

So it's up to the YHA. Up because the city of Bath sits in a hollow with a ring of hills around it and the hostel is near the summit of one of them. Looking at a map, I have no inclination to walk there with suitcase and backpack. But since the uni is nearby on the same slope and there are plenty of buses serving the students, I head to the town stop, board a bus and get off ten minutes later at the hostel.

There's a nice, although steep drive, which curves from road to premises. I drag myself and gear up this and at the top get the first glimpse of where I will be staying for three nights. It's impressive; a classy looking villa in the Italian style. On further exploring of building and surrounds, I form the opinion that this is the best hostel of my entire half-year odyssey.

At check in, there's some minor linguistic difficulty when my attempt at humour is mis-taken by the non-English reception girl

* * *

The thing about Bath, which distinguishes it from Bristol, is that this is a town which has money. There are many fine buildings, occupied by fine people, with fine incomes. Ergo, they are the ones who dictate how the town is going to be, and what they do not want is the grot which characterises a great deal of Brizzle.

Little litter, no bins blocking pavements, cars not parked any old place the owners choose and hallaylooyah no grotfiti.

Question: why do I usually stay in Br. When Ba. is clearly more to my taste?

Answer: along with Bath's refinement are higher prices, a limited choice of hostels (3) and not much in the way of entertainments.

This latter will be disputed by some because there is a theatre, cinema, and a smattering of Meetup groups, but put against Bristol's offerings these are a puny selection. Once again it's that inescapable nemesis of the ambitious; **Y**ou **C**an't **H**ave **E**verything.

* * *

More about Fat Kevin

I climb the stairs up to my room, which is generously sized and only has 6 bunks, (practically empty by the standards I've become used to), and on one of the beds is a older gent of heavy build and unhealthy mien

'Didn't we meet in the Bristol YHA?', I say to him. He shows no sign of recognition. 'You were just off to South America'. This he does acknowledge.

A hospital issue crutch – just one, not a pair - leans against the end of the bed. There may be a medical justification for this, but that's not why big K has it. He explains later when we are sitting in the large and pleasant kitchen/dining room.

'When they see the crutch at airports or when boarding liners it gets you priority. I don't walk down miles of corridors; they fetch me a wheelchair and someone to push it.' In this there is a hint that Kevin has a bit of a selfish side. Another thing he says tends to confirm.

He's attended the same Bristol doctors surgery as me and they have prescribed him an item that I too was given. It's a large bottle of skin cream. I told him that I left mine in the place where most of my belongings are stored since it was too heavy and bulky to carry around. Kevin says 'I threw it away'.

In deep gratitude to the NHS for the care that they have given me and awareness that they don't have adequate funding, chucking away medical and related items is a bit of an affront. Doesn't bother Kevin apparently. Seeing as he looks to be one heart attack away from the morgue, you might think that Kevin would have some respect for the NHS and its dedicated, skilled staff.

One night we sit in the lounge and demolish two bottles of wine which he pays for. I contribute a small bottle of smuggled-in vodka. Alcohol does its usual fine job of boosting bonhomie and we are in agreement about much, especially on the topic of wives. Kevin has a line which all men would be well advised to ponder before entering matrimony, 'You find someone, end up hating them, then you give them a house'.

Next day once the liver has done its vital work, K is not as amiable. We're discussing food in shops and he remarks that all food has a sell-by date. I dispute this, since some products are either ageless or actually improve as time goes by. My contradiction has a dramatic effect. Kevin says,

'Well that's the end of that discussion', and he means it. It's his way or no way. Since I don't have much sympathy for the dogmatic, he's right, the conversation is over.

That's no great loss, he may be clever but he's ugly, self-centred and bad tempered. He was right about wives and houses though.

* * *

The All Hallows nutters

Raha - She came in through the kitchen window (Remember the Beatles song? Wikipedia has an explanation for the lyric). Raha does not work at fifteen clubs a day, although she does have the figure for a dancer.

This is what happened:

It's early, I'm sitting at the one decent table there is in All Hallows. The other one in the sort-of common room is wobbly and the single chair next to it is seven eighths demolished – its top rail missing, the leg joints with ominously wide gaps - one good kick away from being firewood.

That room is favoured by most residents so it's not a quiet workspace. My present location isn't perfect either since the table gets used for late night snacking and there's usually the remains, featuring smears of ketchup, adhering to the table top.

Dee, the housekeeping lady tells me, 'They ought to know to clean up after themselves', and I agree with her. But oughtfullness is not doing the trick; 'ought' doesn't work with low-emotional intelligence people.

A man, originally from Djibouti, tells me that he knows the appropriate conventions since he has spent much of his life in the Netherlands; he has 'European values' - shame this is not general.

So I do a table clean-up, make myself coffee and get down to some keyboard time. At 6:45 in the morning, the only sounds to be heard are bird advertising. That's the purpose of chirpy avian noise – they are sending lonely heart messages using the original form of twitter.

This can be successful; a few days ago, a sparrow was sitting on the corner of the kitchen roof and broadcasting his offer at good volume. The next time I looked up, he wasn't alone, he'd pulled a tasty bird – a female, I trust – and they were busy in an intimate way, delicto flamenco as I've heard it called.

I point this out to Dee, who is sitting nearby having a fag. 'Aw, the dirty little buggers', says she.

With all this tweeting going on of a morning, you'd expect an explosion of the birdy population, unfortunately reports in the media suggest otherwise. Anyways, bird song doesn't distract me from my early day typing sessions; I am occupied with my magnum opus which is creeping towards being done.

And then there is a CRASH.

It came from the kitchen and I can't think of any explanation, there's no machinery in operation. It is an empty, lifeless kitchen in which nothing is happening. Did a meteorite, a piece of space junk land on the roof? Or worse?

> A man was sunbathing in his London garden when a body hit the ground feet away from him. It was a stowaway who fell off a Kenya Airways flight from Nairobi last week as the plane approached London's Heathrow Airport. The person, who authorities have not named, didn't survive.
> Most stowaways don't. Over 77% of the people who have attempted to hitch an illegal ride on an aircraft have died, the Federal Aviation Administration said. At least 126 people have tried it since 1947. **CNN report**

Three, perhaps four seconds later and this question is answered; Raha, the lanky Somalian woman bursts through the door behind me and makes high-speed transit towards the main part of the building. I catch a couple of words delivered in flight. 'Lost my keys'.

Now with some facts and a proffered rationale – I attempt to assemble a coherent sequence.

- Raha wishes to enter house
- Raha cannot find keys

- Raha goes into yard behind neighbouring house and scales fence
- Raha sees open kitchen window
- Raha bounds through window onto sink draining board
- This landing creates much noise

Yes, that seems reasonable. Except that next to me the door to the back garden is open and was fully available for Raha's ingress. Perhaps in Somalia windows are more convenient entry points rather than doors. Never having visited that land, I cannot say.

It's not often in my life that people come in through the window, so if you asked me what I would estimate the odds to be of it happening again a few hours later, I'd be suggesting the order of number which applies to winning the lottery.

But if you read any book on probability you find that apparently-unlikely things can happen and it is reasonable to anticipate them. For example, in roulette, if black comes up 6 times in a row, you might think, this can't go on much longer, red is becoming increasingly probable. Then you bet and if necessary bet again a time or two on red.

Don't do that; there's a name for this practice, it's called The Gambler's Fallacy. Put simply, if there is no imbalance to the roulette wheel and the outcome of each roll is perfectly random, then for each throw, the result is equally likely to be of either colour. Although devoutly wished-for, the preceding history brings no magic force to bear.

Reduce the situation to absurdity – a useful thought-experiment-testing-tool. Imagine that you have seen red come up 17 times. On the next throw, just as with the first, thirteenth and twenty sixth, or any other number including 1001, the result can be either red or black, entirely uninfluenced by what has happened before. (Please don't whinge to me about the house advantage slot)

End of lecture.

With that said, perhaps one should consider it entirely reasonable to expect that a person-entering-through window event may occur again within a proximate time.

And it did.

2:00 a.m. I'm asleep when the crash and shouting two doors away wakes me. Loud, angry words are being exchanged. The resident of the room in question was asleep. He mentions this to the bod who has just infenestrated. The latter party offers the excuse, 'Lost me keys mate, sorry' and goes on to say that he also regrets choosing the wrong window.

These apologies do not much soothe the rightful occupant who proposes a punch up the bracket as equaliser. Discussions and counter offers continue at volume for several minutes before calm resumes and this witness goes back to sleep.

* * *

Breakfast, Richard, and big bellies

The kitchen and dining area of the Rock 'n Bowl is large. There is a table big enough to accommodate a dozen or so people if they sit tidily; they usually don't. Shifts occupy it according to the hour and nationality. Early mornings, six-ish, it will be serious workers. They are busy making flasks of tea and lunchtime sandwiches, one eye on the clock. In the main they are from the East, Romania, Russia, Poland.

By seven, the first beginnings of those with less pressing schedules, mostly older bods, perhaps some tourists about to make an excursion requiring an early start. The microwave and the toaster see some action.

And now is the hour when staff begin to set out the apparatus and supplies for the 'included free' breakfast, which according to your perspective is about as basic as it gets, or if you have just left a prison bread-and-water regime, rich and varied – bread, no change there, but now with mini butter-in-foil packages and jam. There are flakes of corn, elemental muesli, milk and – hallelujah - real made-with-actual-beans coffee. This a rare luxury in hostels, normally it's instant of the cheapest-bulk-type-we-could-find. I can't drink that stuff.

As the hour moves on, types who more represent the mainstream begin to show up and some stove and frying pan action will begin, probably versions of our nation's distinctive fast-breaker – the full cooked. This takes time to prepare and consume, there is no hurry, and conversation may begin; a principal theme being adventures of the previous night.

Towards noon, Spanish can be heard since the Iberian natives have begun to surface. When there are only two or three of them, they speak in nothing louder than a shout. Fill the room with español-hablantes and conversation for reserved individuals is impossible.

It's not just the mega-volume chat, there's also the Latin music. The poor dears need it, they gotta have it. There's a flat screen TV on the wall and if you know which end of a remote control to point with you can select your preferred españopop. The TV audio may be in competition with other soundz coming from a smart phone/Bluetooth speaker combo – *muy popular* these days, music is *muy bien, verdad?*

* * *

Scene: same place **Hour:** mid-evening

Eating done for the day, I am sitting talking to a resident-of-the-third-kind. He doesn't fit the category of minimum-wager, nor is he a tourist. Richard tells me that staying overnight in Bristol suits his work visiting locations throughout the South West to fix things mechanical and electrical.

The company he works for offers a range of motorised toys for company fun-days. I expect you have some idea of what I'm talking about; a company takes its team out for a day of fun/motivation 'n bonding.

Because I'm having difficulty understanding exactly what Richard does he shows me some video clips on his phone. They are of radio controlled model vehicles the size of small to large suitcases. Some just about big enough to sit on. These devices are running around a terrain with peaks, troughs and mud. I can see how operating these models can be fun – for about half an hour.

There are other items that companies can choose for their fun-day; Richard's firm has a menu of motorised big-boy-toy-ware. A farmer friend of mine does the same sort of thing when he's not raising sheep. He offers hovercraft or quad bike driving around his property. He's got his son with him to help run the events and repair things which break. Exactly what my new acquaintance Richard does a lot of.

He can't get enough of this electro-mechanical fixing; at home he's not slumped in front of the box like half the population, instead he's in his workshop busy with more making and repairing. He showed me video of miniature steam engines which he has built or improved. 'I bought this one on eBay, but I didn't like some of the small screws the original maker had used, so I turned some new ones in brass – they look better.'

I used to read 'Model Engineer magazine' in my teens, so I knew what I was looking at and the huge amount of time, skill and patience it takes to do work of this type.

'Richard you are a genius', I told him. He is a modest man who says that his hearing isn't good – he didn't respond to my remark, perhaps it wasn't audible. Rather, he's a do-er, doesn't look for more than the satisfaction of using his skill making things to very high standards.

Somewhat surprisingly to me, he has a guitar with him and he tells me he's learning. I give it a try and find it difficult to hold, it keeps slipping away from me. I tell Richard that I have the same trouble with the guitar I had in my last real home. He puts it to me bluntly, 'It's your belly that's in the way'. That had never occurred to me before, now I can't forget it.

* * *

New measurement system

Surely there are few people left in the Western World who have not noticed that we are becoming fat. Pieces in the media talk about it, celebrities opine, experts purport to know what to do about it – it's a live topic. But one thing is missing so far - we haven't got a satisfactory measure for belly size.

It's a bit tricky; measuring the circumference of a body at belly height, gives you one piece of data, but on its own it's insufficient, what is needed is a measure of the volume. And I think that I have spotted a way to express this.

If you buy a car these days the spec. will tell you such things as motor power Kw(atts), distance you can go on a full tank and . . . the size of the boot.

Whether on foot or in car boots are not easy to measure, the shape is too irregular. Bellies are the same, so what applies for automobile boots might work for humans.

Outdoor suppliers offer rucksacks sized by the litre volume of contents that they can hold for the same reason, so let us size bellies the same way. Full disclosure: I compared my belly to a 10L rucksack, the bag is bigger.

* * *

About Bristol

I have mixed feelings about Bristol, the facilities for practical matters are very good but for me the aesthetics are dismal. For a city with such a vast history, Bristol is an ugly mess. I'm talking about the look of the town, the optics.

The problem is in two parts, modern day grot, and the lack of respect for the old buildings. There are areas in which fragments from the past remain, but they are overwhelmed by the far greater amount of post-war brutal/utility construction.

* * *

History of Bristol - in just the minimum keywords

Palaeolithic era
Stone Age
Iron Age
Roman settlement
Saxon burgh of Brycgstow
Anglo-Saxon slave trade
1066 Norman conquest
14th century Bristol England's third-largest town after London and York
15–20,000 inhabitants
1348–49 Black Death
1453 End of the Hundred Years War

Cod, new-found-land
1497 John Cabot discovered America
1498 Cabot set sail with five ships and never returned
1588 Bristol sent three ships against Spanish Armada
1642 First English Civil War
Royalist troops captured Bristol on 26 July 1643
Recaptured for Parliament during English Civil War
Oliver Cromwell ordered destruction of castle
17th and 18th centuries, transatlantic slave trade
Industrial Revolution
Construction of floating harbour
1801 Population 61,000, 19th century - grew five-fold

Geography

On tidal River Avon
Bristol town founded on hill between Rivers Frome and Avon
Sea connections to Wales, Ireland, Iceland, France, Spain, Portugal
c. 1247 Stone bridge built across the Avon,
1240 and 1247 a Great Ditch constructed to straighten out River Frome
The long passage up tidal Avon Gorge made port secure during Middle Ages
- but became a liability later
Construction of new "Floating Harbour" 1804–09 failed to overcome
Bristol lies on lesser coalfield
17th century collieries opened Bristol, North Somerset, South Gloucestershire

Trade

Wool, fish, wine and grain during Middle Ages

Trade across the Atlantic developed
13th century Bristol becomes a busy port
Woolen cloth, wine from Gascony, Bordeaux, principal import
From Ireland fish, hides, cloth probably linen
Exports to Ireland broadcloth, foodstuffs, clothing and metals
Trade with Waterford and Cork, also Portugal, Iceland
Bristol's merchants look West for new sources of cod fish
- abandon Iceland late-15th century, imported freeze-dried cod called 'stockfish'
Overseas trade increased late 15th, 16th centuries
Mid-16th c. imports from Europe, wine, olive oil, iron, figs, dried fruits, dyes.
- Lost access to Gascony wines. Imports of Spanish, Portuguese wines increased
Exports cloth cotton and wool lead and hides
Slave trade, consequent demand for cheap brassware for export to Africa
- caused boom in copper, brass manufacturing industries of Avon valley
- Encouraged progress of the Industrial Revolution

Exploration

1481 explorers may have discovered Grand Banks, Newfoundland, rich in cod
1497 John Cabot, sponsored by Henry VII, looking for new route to Orient discovered North America.

Slavery

Over 2000 slaving voyages made by Bristol ships between late 17th century and abolition in 1807

Rapid 18th-century expansion of Bristol's part in the "Triangular trade" in Africans taken for slavery in the Americas

Anti-slavery campaigners, inspired by John Wesley, started campaigns against the practice

Industry

Advances in shipbuilding

Further industrialisation, glass, paper, soap, chemicals, sugar, in Avon valley

Bristol terminus of the Great Western Railway

1793 Disruption of maritime commerce through war with France

1807 Abolition of slave trade contributed to city's failure to keep pace with newer manufacturing centres of the North and Midlands

Cotton industry failed to develop in the city

Sugar, brass and glass production went into decline

Brunel designed Great Western Railway between Bristol and London, two pioneering Bristol-built steamships, the SS Great Western and the SS Great Britain, and the Clifton Suspension Bridge

At end of 19th century main industries tobacco, cigarette manufacture, paper, engineering

Early 20th century, Bristol forefront of aircraft manufacture

21st century becoming important financial and high tech hub. Bristol population now nearly half a million

If that doesn't impress you, compare it with the history of the USA, which will fit nicely on the back of a postcard.

* * *

I don't like:

- ☹ The Bearpit, a sunken plaza notorious for druggies and muggings.
- ☹ The shortage of and competition for housing and the high rents.
- ☹ Messy front gardens, full of chucked-out furniture, dismantled cabinets, fast food packaging, weeds.
- ☹ Dustbins and recycling bins which block the pavements.
- ☹ Cars parked on the pavements, making it hard for pedestrians.
- ☹ Traffic driving at way over the speed limit.
- ☹ Cyclists riding on the pavements – often at high speed, making for dangerous collisions with pedestrians.
- ☹ Ugly, and to me meaningless, graffiti on almost every formerly blank wall.
- ☹ Litter, in parks, even in childrens' play areas.
- ☹ Broken bottles on pavements and in the road.
- ☹ The layout of The Centre, with so much traffic on the roads coming to it making it difficult to cross roads to get to the central area.
- ☹ Poor driving - many drivers are recent immigrants from countries where standards differ from the UK.
- ☹ Main traffic arteries cross through the town centre increasing pollution, traffic jams and collisions.
- ☹ The still and dirty water of the floating harbour

- ☹ Council properties of uninspired design, poor construction and inadequate maintenance.
- ☹ Big square office buildings with designs which have no relation to one another or historic structures.
- ☹ Air pollution from vehicles - especially bad in The Centre area.
- ☹ So many people smoke cannabis that you smell it most of the time in public places.
- ☹ The attempt to make Bristol a tourist destination. The city is already too full, disrespects its history and the recent Harbourside leisure developments encourage yobbish behaviour at weekends.
- ☹ Stokes Croft, plastered with ugly graffiti and fly-posting.
- ☹ Girls with extensive acreages of tattoos, much metalwork in their faces and hanks of hair which a rope maker would reject as sub-standard.
- ☹ Girls who avoid eye contact – there seems to be a distinct Bristol sub-species.
- ☹ The price of beer in most pubs.
- ☹ Skateboarders disrespecting the war memorial.
- ☹ Vandalised 'YoBikes (rental bikes) abandoned here there everywhere.
- ☹ 'The Fountains', less a 'feature', more a shallow puddle obstacle for pedestrians.

I'm not in love with this town. Certainly there are compensations, but the apparent lack of civic pride upsets my sensitive soul.

One of the first things you see when entering Bristol by road is 'The Bearpit', a sunken plaza which showcases exactly what is wrong with Bristol.

What particularly gets me is that evidently there has been an attempt to create a pleasant green space here with attractive planter/raised bed thingies. But these structures now neglected accommodate a few hardy veg plants - mostly leafy greens - and a jungle of weeds, fag packets, cider cans and one presumes condoms (used) and hypodermics (ditto).

Ugly, ugly, ugly. Very.

How could Bristol town planners think it a good idea to funnel heavy traffic through the heart of the town and past this eyesore?

Halfway between Bearpit and Harbourside is a paved-area-with-embellishments known as The Centre - the name demonstrating the same lack of imagination and taste as the actual site. It's hard surfaced throughout except for an area with small stainless steel boxes which are the nozzles for a water spraying feature termed 'The Fountains'. If you want to see a pukka fountain, take a trip to Rome or Geneva, the Bristol puddle is to those magnificent examples what Pound stores are to Harrods.

(Update, July – there is a modest flow of water now, hardly a true fountain). This whole space could have been an attractive park/island at the heart of the city but no; the reality is a mess of pavement, a few stranded plain trees and stalls selling burgers and kebabs.

At the far end stands a memorial to the dead of two world wars. It is at the head of a plaza popular with skateboarders. More bad planning; I'm all for the yoof having fun and developing skill, but not disrespecting a monument which invites quiet reflection on history, tragedy and sacrifice.

There's an area adjacent to the Harbourside strip of restaurants and bars which is dedicated to funfairs and, in winter, ice skating. That could be a place for skateboarders to enjoy as much noisy fun as they want without disturbing anyone.

The current site of their activity, in front of the memorial is grossly incompatible with its solemn purpose. A recent episode took the affront further; a skateboarder wrenched apart one of the benches which surround this plaza to make an obstacle for his jumping manoeuvres. That made the local news and was sufficient provocation for the Council to take action.

The roads forming the top and bottom boundaries of The Centre stream with buses, cars, trucks and bikes; this is not a pedestrian-friendly area, in part because the use of bicycles is accepted in areas primarily intended for foot traffic. As far as I am aware, this tolerance is peculiar to Bristol, in other cities it's an offence.

I like to cycle, but I'm not going to risk it in Bristol; too dangerous (and hilly).But many others are bolder, good for them. I support forms of transport alternative to the private car – if ever it should be needed to demonstrate the disadvantages of a one car: one person society, this locale is ideal.

Throughout Bristol bikes are everywhere - parked, lying on their sides, thrown into bushes, hurtling at your front and back, on the pavements and weaving through stalled traffic. Bike city it is. Or rather I wish it were (appropriately managed) because they don't make the air stink or park on pavements.

Bicycles are not a solution entirely green and pure; bikes + rider do kill people occasionally – a recent case was of a man on a 'fixed-wheel' bike who collided with and terminated a London pedestrian. I have had several too close encounters, you can't hear them coming and athletic types on racing style bikes travel at considerable speed - enough kinetic energy to do damage.

The Bristol to Bath ex-railway path is a location where accidents can be predicted with certainty. The mix of walkers, some with prams, and cyclists of all types and velocities travelling in opposing directions on a narrow track – exactly the ingredients for people getting hurt.

Although it is very pleasant to have greenery to both sides in the heart of the city, this is not a place to relax in view of the danger of death or mutilation by high speed bike-missile.

Next disappointment for me is the water, that of the floating harbour. It's static and unappealing, you will never see me jumping into it however intoxicated or overheated. This is dead water, it's not just resting, it is deceased just like the famed Norwegian Blue. (Monty Python - try and keep up please).

This water is going nowhere; the reason for holding it captive is sound; if it weren't constrained by a lock, it would come and go twice a day and do so in a fashion leaving no doubt. The Bristol channel by reason of its shape has enormous tides. There is indication of this if you look down into one of the associated locks when the tide is out; on one side there is water not too distant from your feet and on the other a gaping void with nothing until you look down, down, down deep. At the bottom will be a small flow of water escaping from leaks in the lock gates. You'd want to the latter to be built nice and strong because they hold back a serious tonnage of the wet grey stuff.

* * *

It's a curious thing that up until the nineteen thirties, houses built en masse were rather attractive - not particularly functional by today's standards - but a whole lot more stylish and carefully built than what followed post WW2.

I realise that wartime bombing caused much damage and that replacement housing was urgently needed but that justification is becoming old 73 years on. In any case it's no excuse for day-to-day neglect by citizens and the authorities.

The early 20th century, at origin 'utility', dwellings are nearing their expiry dates. You could inject loadsa money into mass renovation and for sure that would improve the cosmetics but it won't fix the central issue which is that peoples' standards and expectations have changed. We desire the IKEA lifestyle in an environ which is spacious, not poky.

Given that a lot more people live in this city than it comfortably holds, residents inevitably occupy less space - instead of a house, an apartment; instead of the latter, a room; instead of a room to yourself; you share it - 'hot bedding'; instead of two-to-a-room; a hostel and now you are one of 12, stacked three high, floor to ceiling.

You doubt this? Read my account - 'Hostel Hell'. Oh, you are.

There's not much in this existence-as-experienced-by-humans which is indisputable, so if it makes you happy, my opinions are wrong, and yours are right.

But before you spontaneously combust, review the list below, it may calm you.

What's good about Bristol

I like:

- ☺ The Bristol Royal Infirmary
- ☺ It's a cosmopolitan town; you can meet people from everywhere
- ☺ For me, a very good bus service
- ☺ St Nicholas Market and its ethnic cafes and stores
- ☺ Loads of pubs – including eight Wetherspoons.

- ☺ The independent shops of Gloucester Road and East Street, Bedminster
- ☺ Cider
- ☺ Bristol Sweet Mart and Malik's
- ☺ Numerous stalls selling fresh fruit and veg
- ☺ The food banks and free food places for the homeless
- ☺ (Some) attractive front gardens
- ☺ The major church architecture – St. Mary Redcliffe, Bristol Cathedral
- ☺ Proximity to other interesting places, Bath, Cardiff, seaside etc
- ☺ Many green spaces
- ☺ Some ancient and imposing trees
- ☺ The Central Library reading room
- ☺ Bristol University and Art Gallery/Museum
- ☺ All things Banksy
- ☺ Lots of young people and students
- ☺ Many live music venues and other entertainments

* * *

Next is an example of a service I obtained in Bristol which was effective and delivered in a user-friendly manner. Much appreciated!

Advice for Citizens

When a citizen needs advice, who should advise him – wait I know the answer to this one, Google, right?

Google does know a lot, can't be denied. But some folk haven't got a Googletron, so they can't find out what big G thinks, and others are looking for more than even a really expensive G-tron can provide; hand holding.

I was one of the second type and conventional thinking had got me nowhere near a solution to my nasty problem. It had been going on for a very long time; I can't recall to the nearest year even, but at least a decade. And it was costing me a lot of money, when I only had coming in what British welfare provides.

My business life has been up and down, there have been times when I even felt rich, sort of, many more when that whirring noise that ATMs make just before spitting out banknotes was the sound of heaven being kind to an idiot. Those were some of the few moments when I might have been persuaded into religious belief.

Specifics: I remember the moment it all began; I was sitting in my car at Prestwick airport, Scotland and using an early mobile phone to call my bank. I wanted to ask for an overdraft. To my surprise they agreed without being difficult to lend me £3,000.

That dealt with my immediate need; what it was is now forgotten; might have been to pay wages, since I had three employees or it could have been fees for the private school my children went to. At the time I felt relieved that the pressure was off, but I had no inkling of what that phone call was going to cost over the years, reckoned in worry and pounds sterling.

That blasted overdraft stuck with me forever and ever, right up until my arrival in Bristol and then some. Every month around fifty pounds interest was debited from my bank account. I was never flush enough to pay the overdraft off. So the total amount of cost over all the years was near enough twice the sum borrowed. Ten per cent of my small income went to the bank every month. It was finally the moment for this ostrich to remove his head from sand and get help.

I don't think I even bothered asking big G because I wasn't looking for the good and sensible, what I wanted was a more streetwise and ingenious fix.

Now you might think that the Citizens Advice service, which is to be found in towns all over the British Isles, would be bound to guide guidees in the right, proper, authorised and impartial manner to resolve difficulties. Maybe I was a lucky exception because I was given help which was weighted heavily in my favour, not the lender's.

You'll understand that here I shall be protecting my helper, I'll call her Jay, and that is not his real name.

From the get-go, Jay was friendly and concerned to have my problem sorted. The route was to make it clear to the bank that taking £50 a month from my account leaves me insufficient to live on. If that could be shown, then a mechanism could be used which reduces the amount payable to a token sum, just a pound or so.

Step one is to build a statement of income and outgoings. All you clever accountant types will think you know how to do this – you'd be wrong. As Jay said, 'This is more an art than science'. What was meant by that remark is start with the end result and then enter data which delivers it.

I wasn't expecting this and my preparation for the task was a review of my bank statements and the assignment of items to appropriate categories, more a list than a proper spreadsheet.

Jay began plugging my items and costs into a form for this purpose. The result of the first try was unsatisfactory, I wasn't broke enough. Jay asked me about other outlay which I perhaps hadn't considered and forgotten purchases and costs came back to mind and were added in. The result after a couple of iterations of this process demonstrated that I could barely cover my living expenses, hence unable to pay any further interest.

The form was printed off, I signed it and, as my highest priority once out of the CitsAdv office, despatched the letter at the nearby post office.

Big relief. Big thanks to Jay.

* * *

But I haven't finished with what's bad about Bristol, here's the next moan. I have stayed in all the backpacker hostels in Bristol bar one – the Full Moon. The reason I didn't go there is that the reception staff in that place suggested that I wouldn't like it. They were probably right, it features late night loud rock concerts and I'd had enough of that at the

Rock 'n Bowl. However all the hostels have deficiencies as you'll see reported in the following.

Here are reviews left on sites such as Hostelworld.com of bad hostels in Bristol

The 007 Backpackers Hostel

Elsewhere I have described the 007 Backpackers hostel as the worst in Bristol. To support my opinion, here are posted reviews from others who have stayed there.

New Zealand, Couple, 18-24

"I would rate this a 0 if I could, it is a false advertisement, its location is miles out of the city in a not very nice suburb, the outside of it looks like a old run down drug house, the inside, atmosphere and people there all reflect this and we felt like we were in a halfway house. We didn't feel safe AT ALL and left in the middle of the night to sleep uncomfortably in an airport, but I much preferred that to spending another second in this place. You couldn't pay me to stay there!"

* * *

Belgium, Male, 31-40

"Worse place to stay ever. Trust me I felt like I'm in some movie about gangsters. Booked there for two days I arrived there ate something and washed my dishes, I sat and the owner came and told in a tone of giving orders "dry the dishes and put them there". I said I'm not going to do that now. She phoned her father and mother came with a car and shouting you have to leave and no refund, .inside

atmosphere looks like a movie called Shutter Island. Don't go there, you might get hurt by the owners."

* * *

Australia, Male, 25-30

"Horrible hostel, im not usually one to write a review but goddamn i havent stayed in a worse hostel yet, hostel is full of live ins which kills the vibe because you constantly feel like you are unwanted guest in someone elses house, security is bad, people steal your food, beds a super uncomfortable, showers are crap and the whole bathroom stinks all the time, any way dont stay here."

* * *

USA, Male, 18-24

"The hostel was dirty, unkempt, and the carpets smelled of mildew. The 2nd night I got locked out. NO ONE INFORMED ME OF A CURFEW. I tried getting in a quarter after midnight. You'd think that's reasonable for a hostel in a thriving town like Bristol. After walking all night to keep warm, I got back at 5:30a, and a staff member let me in. He asked me to wait because he mopped the floors. THE FLOORS WEREN'T EVEN WET. HOW TOTALLY INHUMANE AND DISRESPECTFUL."

* * *

Here is the review I ultimately posted about this outpost of hell:

This is the worst hostel in Bristol - avoid it.
The shabby front door of the 007 Backpackers hostel is a foretaste of what is inside, which can be summed up as a low grade hostel with owners who only care about one thing - taking your money. This place was once a hostel for homeless people, it has been barely updated since. Many of the occupants are long stayers. In the kitchen the stove is barely functional and food storage limited. The shower is "prison block" style with no separation between the stalls. The lavatory has no lock. There's no soap, towel and the two hand dryers are not connected electrically and don't work. At the rear of the "dining area" there is a room used for additional food storage and the door to the outside is permanently open - there are plenty of rats in Bristol, so beware. The one good point the employed staff are generally nice people and very helpful. Although the hostel is outside of the town, the bus service is frequent. At best this is a place to stay for one night if you are heading to the airport in the morning. Otherwise avoid.

Date of stay: January 2019

I should point out that there are quite a lot of positive reviews of the 007. So if my criticism is fair, how is it possible that others have much different opinions? I think this is down to some compound of luck, short stays, inexperience or the contrary, having encountered utterly gross conditions elsewhere.

* * *

The Old Port House is also terrible, possibly even worse, but as you will read, I never saw any hostel staff while there and depending on what they are like, good or bad, the O.P.H. might even eclipse the 007

* * *

My review:

Title: **'Uniquely horrible'**

The positives: location is very central, everything you need is nearby. In the room I had there were single (non-bunk) beds.

The problems: they started with the fact that the hostel is not easy to locate, the name 'Old Port House' is not to be seen outside, they have changed it locally but not on the website. During a four-day stay I never saw any staff person. There was no one in reception when I arrived so I never checked-in or out. The first unpleasant thing I encountered was the handrail on the stairs - sticky with grease or something. The bed had a mattress with springs poking into my back. The noise from revellers in the street continued into the first hours of the next day. The bathroom, which is shared with another dorm was horrible - overflowing lavatories leaking across the bathroom floor and no toilet paper. There was no secure storage for luggage. The next door dorm looked like a scene from hell. If you have any other possibility don't stay here.

Date of stay: October 2018

* * *

My credentials for making these statements: I have travelled widely for over 50 years and in the last two have stayed in 33 hostels across 9 countries. My objective when reviewing is to offer impartial description to other travellers so that they can choose places they will enjoy.

In the third world you need to anticipate from time to time encountering toilets full to overflowing, bed bugs, filthy sheets, night-time predators, robbery. I have seen all these and it won't surprise me if others can top my experiences.

Even in the western world a few problems are inherent in hostel stays - it's luck of the draw whether other guests behave well or not. And until there is a world database listing snorers so that they can be kept well away from other guests, you can reckon that around one in ten of your dorm neighbours will be an offender.

Of course you don't have to stay in hostels, alternatives range from select hotels at fancy prices, to a nice piece of cardboard under a flyover - your choice. Or as Duncan, a now dead friend, put it 'Get a shopping cart and a tarpaulin and you have a mobile home'.

* * *

And now here is another ugly aspect of the Bristol scene.

Light body damage

If you are in the market for a vehicle with light body damage, Bristol's a good place to look; about every tenth car or van has a dent or scuffed paint. The conditions here favour collisions;

- ☹ Main traffic arteries cross through central areas of the town
- ☹ Many drivers are recent immigrants from countries where standards differ from the UK.
- ☹ There is a bling (not to say 'drug') culture in which young men buy fancy cars and drive them energetically
- ☹ Lots of the neighbourhood streets are narrow with room for only one vehicle at a time
- ☹ Despite law and penalty for infraction, mobile phone use by drivers continues

In my short time living in Easton, I have seen two collisions occur in front of me, some near misses, and loadsa sparkly fragments of car reflector lenses evidencing bang crash wallop.

Waiting for the routinely unpunctual 506 bus, I see courier vans and young men in flash cars driving at well over the speed limit. At the junction of Old Market and Midland Road I was nearly mown down by a car doing - I'd estimate about 60mph - which jumped the just-changed red lights.

Walk along any side street and you will see that vehicles are occupying all possible parking spots. This leaves only a central part of the roadway free for traffic and it has to be one-at-a-time-with-passing-spots, such as you find in country lanes.

These factors make for panel damage or worse. Most common are dents in a front wing, door or hatchback boot panel. Paint scrapes in van sides too. You can see much the same in Paris, too many vehicles, poor driving and an acceptance that banging up your motor is part and parcel of life in a crowded city.

I'm glad I don't own a car

* * *

Untermenschen, zombies and riff raff

If you are unfamiliar with the German word above, it was employed by the Nazis describing people they didn't like and would exterminate if they could. The literal translation is *'under – persons'*.

I am no supporter of fascism or inhumane treatment of anyone, but somehow the German term makes me think of a netherworld populated by creatures which are not fully human – as per Michael Jackson's Thriller video.

And another expression which I wouldn't have chosen myself is *'riff raff'*, this being employed by Chris, a fellow resident in All Hallows. He used it about people who congregate in the Chelsea Inn's back yard. I knew what he meant and it will be difficult to explain it to you without risking the charge of being, snobbish or prejudiced.

Here are some elements, assemble them according to your beliefs and taste:

- clothing in bright colours ☺

- clothing which hasn't seen a washing machine lately ☺

- hair styles from shaven head to waist-length dreadlocks ☺ man-buns ☺

- tattoos and much metalwork embedded on and in body parts, visible and otherwise ☺

- much rolling of self-made cigarettes, with and without additional enhancements ☺

- plenty of talk around conspiracy theories and pseudo-science ☺

- girls sporting curtain-fringe hairstyles ☺

- This in an ambience of dim light, reggae or rap music and blazing bonfire.

Do such characteristics give me reason to dislike such people? No they don't. All I will say is that I don't really fit in with this crowd. I find them welcoming and quite happy to chat with me, but it's never for long because apart from a standard moan about how 'everything is shit', there's not a lot more that we have in common.

I'll just venture one further descriptor, I hate to waste time, all my life I have been busy, trying and sometimes succeeding in developing a project; sometimes to make money, occasionally pro bono publico. (Unfortunately there's little left to attest to this – apart from a couple of restored houses and my scribblings.)

Now I'll take a guess – and this may be an unfair/arrogant assumption – few of the crowd I've been describing have done or are interested in doing comparable things.

The Unbearable Whiteness of Being

If you want to know what Milan Kundera's book title means, ask him; I haven't a clue.

I've been intrigued by the demographic mix one sees in Bristol – I know I have to whisper here, don't want the PC cops nabbing me. What I mean is that walking around my area, Easton, and travelling on the buses you can easily form the impression that there are as many non-white residents as pale-skins.

So much for impressions; my one just mentioned, is wrong by a large margin if you believe what www.bristol.gov.uk has to say. According to that website, just 16% of the local populace belong to a black or minority ethnic group.

Easton presumably doesn't contain an averaged cross section of Bristolians, and logically there exist in other parts vast acreages of monoculture whites to equalise out the stats.

* * *

Fight at the Goose

With a little research – just keeping your eyes open is enough – a modicum of self-organisation and some walking, you don't need to be hungry in Bristol, there's any number of organisations who'll give you something to eat.

In the big, beautiful, ancient and useless (ever-dwindling congregation) St Mary Redcliffe church I found a pile of handy little booklets 'Guide to services for the homeless in

Bristol'. There's a table listing places offering practical services; healthcare, washing – self and clothes - food, addiction help and agencies who offer routes out of homelessness.

Reminiscent of what George Orwell describes in 'Down and Out in Paris and London'; his account of rough living in those towns, the homeless today are also kept on the move, there's no single location providing all you might need. Complain about this and you may be told that 'the gentle exercise of walking is good for you'. A little less so if you have painful ankle and knee joints though.

Rather conveniently for me, there's an establishment which does provide breakfast, lunch and dinner on weekdays. It's halfway between my current abode and the town centre and on a good bus route. You won't need to be long in Bristol before you hear about 'The Goose' - a favourite of the down and out crowd. I've been there for lunch a few times and have no complaints about the grub, it's good and the staff who cook and serve it up are nice people.

There's a light touch of religion - food service begins with grace, and even though I'm a confirmed atheist I'm not going to cavil about that. Minor downsides to dining at The Wild Goose - its full name; fights aren't unusual and it can be hard to find a place to sit and eat, it gets crowded.

You need to be careful what you say and how you behave here as you do in all contact with homeless bods. You can't tell by appearance what they are like in their heads, many are mild-mannered and easy to be with, but others can go ape shit with little warning.

There's been a lot of that in All Hallows recently. I'm not a mental health professional, haven't even read much about it, so I'm only guessing that schizophrenia might lie behind some of the extravagant behaviour I've encountered. I can tell you what the visible signs are; lots of shouting, erratic rushing around and back, much banging of doors, furniture, walls. And need I say, copious swearing?

One lunchtime I was a little early for lunch at The Goose, people were variously hanging around outside, sitting quietly in the eating area and in my case, relaxing in an armchair in the entrance lobby. We had about a quarter of an hour to wait, this time was filled with a spectacle which played out right in front of me, actually rather too close.

A large man of middle age was complaining that another party had hit him. He was bent on revenge, not with more violence – if that could be avoided. His preference was to secure a witness, have the cops attend and press charges.

This was not going as he would have liked; his witness, one of the staff ladies, didn't seem keen on cooperating. Angry man was insistent that she should. Staff lady moved to safe area, an office just behind her. Angry man made an energetic attempt to remove her from this place of refuge.

A couple of male staff engaged and stopped that. Angry man announces to all present the reason why he needs a witness, and in default of that, what action he will be forced to take. 'I'll kill him, so help me' - referring, one presumes to the man who had struck the initial blow.

By this point phones were out and calls to the constabulary made. Perhaps not entirely by coincidence there's a cop shop just around the corner. It didn't take the boys in uniform long to show up. They're used to affray of this sort, their manner relaxed and professional.

The shouting decreased in amplitude and frequency. Then grace and lunch were announced.

Noshing, I looked out of the window and watched the end game - nothing dramatic, a couple of cops, walkie-talkies, a hi-vis police car or two - just an average day at The Goose.

* * *

The air we breathe

Can you remember what a hippie was?

This has exactly what to do with Homeless in Bristol?

Answer, if you shut your eyes, you could be back in Haight-Ashbury, 1967. The smell man; the air was perfumed.

Things have moved on a bit over the intervening half century; what people smoke now is even more pungent and the other aroma of flower-power, patchouli is, fortunately, a distant memory. I really hated how that stuff clung.

And so, while the smell of vapourised tetrahydrocannabinol, might possibly have attracted the 1960s Robert, 50 years on it repels. I don't like it even in small concentrations, which is a problem in areas of Bristol where people congregate.

Sometimes the parts per million is so elevated that there's a chance of a passively obtained high. With doors and windows shut it can still make its way into my quarters and without a supply of bottled air, there's not much alternative to breathing it.

I am definitely getting old, the pleasures have dwindled; jazz and alcohol are all that's left.

* * *

North Street places, pubs & people

For my first Bristol weeks I stayed at the 007 Backpacker's hostel, a horrible place, you will see my review elsewhere. It was the base from which I made the first explorations of my new city.

By looking in meetup.com I found groups of people doing or sharing things that interest me; languages, French and Spanish being two. One such event was coming up and the venue was the intriguingly named Tobacco Factory. I'm not a smoker, but I do like the aroma of cigars, maybe this place of old industry smelled nice.

From West Street, the location of the 007, to North Street is a five minute brisk walk and a twice that hobble. The route takes you along streets of small terraced houses with mostly unkempt front yards, roads with a high curved camber and sidewalks which are 70 percent occupied by motor vehicles, with half of the remaining percentage taken by refuse and recycling bins. Pedestrian-friendly, hardly.

At this point I had no firm mental image of the city's layout. If you had asked me to point to where the North lies and the sun wasn't shining, I wouldn't have had a clue. Now approaching two thirds of a year later, I can have a stab at answering such a question, but this is not a planned city, it is the product of organic evolution and stuff is where stuff wants to be, leave it or take it.

So you wander down a street, cross to another which is at a bit of an angle, repeat a time or two and whatever your internal direction finder was telling you at the outset, now navigation is by guess and hope.

For my present purpose I was looking out for North Street, and despite the roads leading to it not having a right angle intersection between them, persistent progression in roughly the right direction did find me on it after a while. So then, left turn towards the smoking-product works.

What's evident on North Street is that it's an area of changing inhabitants and hence style. This and other districts south of the river were originally housing for workers in Bristol's industries. Now a century and a bit later, the old manufacturings are gone, large work halls and workers counted in the thousands are no more. The houses remain; coal fires, privies and tin baths replaced with mod cons – central heating, designer bathrooms, kitchens, furnishings from IKEA, pesto and humus in the fridge.

The new occupants won't be returning from work with dirty hands, stained clothing and gasping for a pint of brown ale.

'Chardonnay or Pinot Grigio? We're out of Barollo.'

Yip, yap, yuppification.

The shops, restaurants and pubs reflect this and are of quite different character to those on West Street where I stay. Continuing on towards the Tobacco Factory, I pass a pleasant looking pub with flyers advertising upcoming music events. There's also a menu – its prices off-putting to me.

From there on, descending the hill -some way below, at the bottom, is the river - it's alternately bistro, wine bar, deli, fancy baker a solitary late night shop and finally I make out the TobFac.

This is my first time at the T.F. and I'm a bit early for the language event, so I wander around to have a look. There's the main room, it's big, not football pitch big, just a couple or three tennis courts. There's a long bar at the back of the room but it's not a sit-at bar, people are seated at tables and benches. Off to one side of the entrance is another room, this one is smaller, sort of cosy, all seating taken by parties with pixel-devices and earphones. Later I find that there is also an outdoor space to the rear of the premises.

So now to try and find the foreign language speakers, not easy with no visual clues and amidst loud chatter. I asked at a table or two, 'Meetup?' but they weren't. Eventually I heard babble in many tongues and this was they.

I like to attend language groups so I can chat in French, German or basic Spanish. To do this I need to be able to hear the other party. In crowded pubs this is, or becomes difficult, especially once alcohol does its work.

The girl I am sitting next to is from Iran, but she has been studying in Germany so it is the language of that country we employ. It's interesting but after not very long the volume of background noise annoys too much. So I say *'Tschüß'* and depart.

* * *

Lost, tired, but happy – sort of

The next time I'm on North Street is because I'm heading to the Orchard Inn on Spike Island, they play jazz there on Monday nights. I have been starved of live music for close on a decade, so I am looking forward to this.

As I told you earlier, Bristol is a city which acquired its street layout organically across many centuries; roads go around obstacles not straight through them. Navigation is not by a series of right angle turns so there is some possibility that after a lengthy march you find yourself involuntarily back where you started.

At this point I did not have a smart phone – hence no G-Maps, GPS or similar. Instead I'd made a written note of how far down North Street I should go before branching off into a particular side street, at the top of which I would hit the river road and from there, across a footbridge bringing me close-ish to destination.

Not a route which is all that easy sober, it was to be more difficult later.

I reached The Orchard and thoroughly enjoyed the jazz. But it is now after 10 and that means no chance of a bus back to my digs, last one was half an hour ago. So I attempt to retrace my steps. This begins well, I cross the footbridge and walk along the river road. Exactly where I had joined it from a side street is now unclear; I make a guess and proceed. Bad choice, from now on landmarks are no longer familiar.

The smart thing would have been to turn around and go back to the last definitely known location. A boy scout could tell you that. It is not what I do.

Instead the street I'm on evolves into a section of motorway and eventually, there are direction signs; one gives me some hope that if I persist on this route I will finally return to my home area. A weary mile and a half later, I do. Later looking at a map I see how I went wrong. I was out by just one street when quitting the river road. Bummer.

* * *

Jazz - the blagging of buses - I am from Sweden

I like jazz, especially anything recorded on the Blue Note label ca 1955.

Since Bristol is rich in venues I am perpetually behind the current scene and miss some gigs I would have loved to attend. Despite that, my jazz dosage is brilliant.

Finding The Old Duke and its daily programs of trad jazz didn't take long. That pub is located in one of the areas of Bristol most attractive to visitors and locals; a street with half a dozen other places for a drink and hard by the curiously named stretch of river, Welsh Back.

Next I discovered The Orchard on Spike Island. Monday night is the time to be there. The music format is the simple but versatile 12 bar blues. In fundament all it takes is three chords, but by the time guitar, harmonica or alto have had their way with the melody line you're hearing soulful complexity while your foot, more interested in the bass line, is working loose from its moorings.

The line-up of musicians varies a little from week to week; there's a solid rhythm section – bass guitar, thump box and a rhythm guitar; some classy piano work and in rotation solos from guitar, sax and a blues harp. The playing is very classy; hard to say who is the best musician. If I had to pick just one, I think I'd go for the cat on blues harmonica, man he can bruise a note until it howls.

The core group are joined as the evening progresses by visiting musicians who play and sing the enduring jazz standards.

After the fright I had at Brew Dog, I'm leery about what drink is going to cost, so at the bar I ask 'How much is your cheapest alcohol? No offence is taken at this request; the young barman suggests a cider and I count out small coins in payment.

Looking around the room at the music fans, it's clear that jazz is not favourite among young people, out of perhaps 40 people present, there might be one is less than that number in years and certainly several who are twice.

This night a remarkable thing happens – the lady who is sitting next to me buys me a pint. I may have induced this by offering to get her one then counting out my change in her view and finding that I didn't have enough. I promise to make good on this next time.

If you mention The Orchard to locals, they generally ask, 'Is that the cider pub?' It is, except that as a unique identifier in England's South West, that's about as little use as saying, 'It's a place where you can get a Cornish pasty'.

Getting home is less fun though; although Spike Island is pretty central and a major hub for tourists, with Brunel's famous ship S.S. Great Britain and other attractions, public transport isn't great. The last useful bus for me is well before the close of play at The Orchard, which faces me with the choice of leaving early, or an unwished-for mile walk back to The Centre; the locus for buses to everywhere.

One night I blagged a better solution; I didn't leave the music until it finished and when I reached the nearby bus stop saw that the only remaining buses on the schedule were those from the airport. These ones, while they will pick up passengers from all stops on their route, charge the same flat fare of eight pounds, even if you only want to go part way.

Since one was approaching, I stuck my hand out and waved. It stopped; I boarded and presented my buss pass. This the driver declined, telling me about the pricing as just described. My disappointed expression and motion to get off the bus may have softened his heart, since he then asked 'Where do you want to go?' My answer was 'Just a couple of stops'. These stops however, widely separated; an unpleasant trudge for the time of night and one's physical condition.

Then bus driver he say, 'Alright mate, hop on'. I thanked him profusely, ditto my patron saint - the one who looks out for idiots.

I've said it before and I voice it once again, 'There's a lot of nice people around'.

Another recent discovery; The Left Bank bar - this, located unfortunately in Stokes Croft, an area adored by many, disliked by at least one; this one. I've described it elsewhere, but again in short: tacky, dangerous (traffic) and relatively inaccessible to me coming from my part of town.

But the Left Bank I like, the barman too - he's another jazz aficionado and the music was to my taste on my first visit, last week. Despite the S.C. factor, I will return.

So far, much success in finding the sweet sounds, but not always; I trekked out on a Saturday evening to The Bear in a district called Hotwells. (I enquired about the location's name and apparently the well is as stated, not cold.) My intention was to get an earful of the good stuff. So with dexterous bussing, I made my way to the other side of town, covering the last 100 m on foot. The journey not too difficult, so potentially a repeat venue for me.

The Bear is a modest-looking pub, no shame in that, some of the best keep their charms veiled. I entered and in front of me was a bar and an appropriate number of attached patrons. A bod was being served, so I stood back, demonstrating civilised patience.

Now the bar lady, who I would judge to be a local of standard local properties invites me to order. Instead of doing that, for no reason I can recall, I said in appropriate accent and intonation: 'Hell-Oh, I am from Svee-Den, I have come for the yazz'.

It was a thing of the moment. Why I happened to pick Svee-Den, I can't say, perhaps because I have hair which some people think is blonde. At any rate, the response came, short and disappointing. Bar lady she say, 'There's no jazz for the summer'. I respond, 'This is terrible, it is so long vay back to Stock-holm'.

No sympathy forthcoming, so I left heading for my alternate destination, knowing that friends will be congregating close by at The Nova Scotia. Ten minutes later, sitting with them on a bench outside the pub, alongside a harbour basin full with small yachts I recount the Sveedish moment at The Bear, 'Very authentic accent' volunteers one of the company.

I thought so too - the wasted talent, I could cry.

* * *

The bars of North Street and an invite

If you want a drink, North Street is a good place to go because there are some attractive bars.

If you want a cheap drink, North Street is a bad place to go.

They're spoiled for me by the über-pricing. Am I prepared to pay a fiver or more a pint? Am I the Emperor of China?

It's so annoying, knowing that c2h5oh is a simple chemical which can be made from inexpensive ingredients.

Leaving aside the argument that the stuff isn't good for you – and there is debate about that - we drinkers are being extorted.

What next, air supplied by Airco.Plc 'from only £3.99 a day*'?   *Subject to acceptance, Terms and conditions apply.

When I say 'bastards', I really mean that.

What the people imbibing expensive juice do for a living I sometimes wonder. There are obviously many for whom these inflated prices are not a concern.

Two days ago I was required to examine my finances and discovered with a shock that booze consumes one quarter of my income. I'm not a drinker of single malt or other spirit at thirty quid a bottle – although I've met some individuals who can empty same in one evening.

No, when I tell the doc that I probably go through fifteen pints a week, I am not unaggerating greatly. (In any case medics probably assume you are and multiply by a factor of at least 1.5).

Here are some of North Street's finest establishments:

The Old Bookshop
That name for a pub would be puzzling if you didn't see that the premises obviously were once what the sign says. Now it is about the trendiest dive of the entire street. Quite what the magic factor is I am unaware and I suppose this

must be a point often analysed by the owners of neighbouring boozodromes.

At any rate, this place is an awkward mix of funny shaped spaces, with a few steps here and there, a small bar with a cute barmaid or two serving and a tiny stage for live music. Weekends it's heaving; so many people cramming themselves in that there's hardly a spot to rest your glass, let alone sit somewhere.

One evening a trio was performing. I thought the singer was Spanish, her pronunciation in that language was impeccable. When I left later on, she and band were outside on the pavement having a smoke, so I asked her. 'I lived in Spain for a couple of years', she told me. Nice looking girl.

Another time in the same bar I had consumed enough of the expensive stuff to start talking to anyone who didn't object. I got chatting to three blokes on a theme connected somehow to one of my standard rants - a reprise of K. Marx's Seeds of Downfall Inherent within Capitalism. (If you have a spare hour sometime, I will be happy to elaborate).

Later as the evening was reaching its end I began the hike back to the appalling 007 hostel where I was staying. There is a warren of little streets you can take and I picked the one which looked least steep – there are a lot of hills in and around Bristol.

So a hobble up said lane, past a park with enclosed dog sniff-and-shit zone and on to a road, about half way to final destination.

'Robert' a voice calls, this surprises me because the chance of anyone knowing me in these parts is slight. But it is I who is being hailed and the addressor is one of the three bods I had been chatting with back in the pub. Turns out that they live not far from my place.

> Bad joke; why do bald men have rabbits tattooed on their head? - From a distance they look like hares.

They invite me back to their place. This is a small house, one of thousand similars. Inside it's compact and pleasant. I'm offered a beer - thank you guys. And stay for half an hour.

* * *

The Leveret

Do you know what a leveret is? It's a young hare. An unusual name for a pub, in this instance, 'bistro' is probably a better word. The interior is freshly re-done in 'designer' tones, lots of shades of not-a real-colour nor definitely white.

The beer is not cheap but below the Brew Dog level of insult. I sit alone, couples are at other tables, ambient noise low. (Note to self - perhaps a venue for a Meetup language group?) On my first visit one beer is enough, nice environ, but no craic.

A second time I encounter Mark, a mild-mannered fellow, who also resides in the 007. I don't know much about him because evenings he sits quietly in the reception/common room headphones on, head down towards a tablet screen – this inhibits conversation.

But now he is at *à table* in this place, beer ready, and I join him. We engage in light chat, he doesn't explain his background, wants to forget it. He's one of the long-termers. Whatever life and/or family that he had before is or are gone. His present and future existence most probably low level institutionalism – money from the state; shared grotty accommodation under aggressive management; food of the basic/takeaway sort; and the outlook – more of the same.

Not much to be joyous about. It could be worse - say and repeat. I hope he gets lucky somehow, some way.

The Record Shop

Knowing now that the Old Book Shop is a pub, it will be less surprising to learn that The Record Shop is one too. It's next door and owned by the same soon-to-be tycoon. A bold move opening two similar emporia immediately next to each other.

I'm there on the grand opening night, not by design, just chance. I come out of the O.B.S. and discover that since about 8 p.m. and the present 10:00 a crowd has formed in and out of the R.S. There are so many people that not only is the pavement full, but the gathering is spilling out into the road.

I make one irresolute attempt to enter and buy beer, but abandon since nine hundred and forty seven people are ahead of me. Handily, there is an open-all-hours store across the road, so I pop over there and buy a quarter of vodka. This keeps me going while I make drunken attempts at chatting up a couple of the local women. Eventually, this palls and I make for home, unsteadily.

* * *

One night in further exploration of West Street, Bedminster, my local area I gave The Albert a try. The sign outside says it has been freshly renovated, which is abnormal for this scruffy area. A hundred yards away is the Black Cat, not renovated and not going to be renovated, ever. Fine just the way it is – beer Monday to Thursday £2.00.

But ever interested to explore new lands, cultures and licensed premises I am prepared to risk one drink *chez* Albert. I get into conversation with the lady behind the bar who might be the owner. I mention that I have been living in Germany and she says that she did too, years ago. This is not uncommon, meeting people who have lived in DE – but not for my reason, I just have itchy feet and like foreign lands.

The explanation this lady gives is the 'partner-in-the army' one. I know the place she is talking about because years ago, when I had just left school and was hitch-hiking around Europe, I visited a schoolmate who had moved to Rheindahlen. In an old archive a photo exists of a young me-with-rucksack, setting off from there about to spend a summer roving around Europe.

I sit down at a table, where there is a couple and get into conversation with them. They're true natives of the area, never been very far from where we are now. Talk gets on to the price of beer and I receive recommendations about places to try where the owners are not too ambitious – or rather, they are smart enough to know that for every punter flush with cash, there are ten who aren't but who still want a drink.

An evening or two later I check out one of the recommends, The Tap and Barrel. For a place of its type, I'm there too early; this is not a pipe-and-slippers-old dude-by-the-fireplace establishment, the signs are clear that the clientele attracted will be the yoof and they attend only when the DJ is set up and blasting big dezibelz.

Before I even get through the front door I pass a phalanx of security heavies. They glance at me, but with no interest, since I don't look anything like the types that they are paid to keep out. Inside, the bar is empty, I wander up to the counter to see what beer is on tap and it's lager, which I will drink only if there's no alternative and you are paying.

Nope, research is now complete, time to head back to the place which dismays - the appalling 007.

* * *

Diverse moments of fun

Matt and Mario, two jolly fellows
One evening in The Commercial Rooms, Corn Street, I had a amusing session with Matt and Mario. The place was crowded and freshly-purchased pint in hand I was looking

for somewhere to sit. Not easy, few perches free. Then I spot a table for four with just two bods at it. I request permission to land and they say OK.

It never takes long before a few words get exchanged in circs like that; we began chatting. M&M were in Bristol for a professional reason, they were doing something at the county court. Exactly what, I never really grasped; it was something about presenting a case on behalf of the Inland Revenue - two words which give me queasy feelings. I couldn't reconcile these two jolly blokes with working for the IR. Just didn't fit.

One parameter was quickly established, neither M nor M was a lawyer. I say 'Huzzah' to that; I've known enough lawyers, was married to one once, and Robert/law-broker compatibility is low. Seems to me that they mostly make their money out of human misery.

Les Ms enquire what I do. This is always tricky since I am in a career limbo, sort of abandoned my former work but not solidly established in that which I hope comes next.

I don't wish to be secretive and really the most convenient thing would be to pretend some common and unremarkable occupation. Years ago, living in a small town near Cambridge, I used to gate crash weekend social functions at the town hall - a chance for some free booze and to meet girls. I used to tell them I was a printer. Worked well, no follow-up questions on that topic.

I must have seemed a bit cagey, M&M became suspicious. Matt said, 'You're a judge'.

'What? Of course I'm not'. That didn't help, they looked at me intently, 'Seen you in court the last time we were here'.

'Impossible, I've only been in Bristol for a couple of weeks.'

They weren't convinced. I changed the subject, asking Mario where he came from. 'Mexico'.

'I spent six months there', I told him and tried a few words of Spanish. Somehow the next English phrase I uttered contained the word 'Notwithstanding'. That did it.

'He is a judge, I knew it', said Matt, Mario thought so too, 'Notwithstanding. Si he is definitely a judge'.

I let it go. The evening continued with more beer, continued accusation and repeated denial - good craic. I hope I bump into them again.

* * *

Christmas was approaching, now I was staying in the Rock 'n Bowl, my highest priority was to obtain, wrap and dispatch presents to my distant children and my granddaughter.

Shopping isn't my thing, I don't like:

- ☹ The smell of shops, neither that of soaps-and-related, nor the odour of plastics or garden chemicals.

- ☹ Lighting either when there isn't enough or when it has that unpleasant bluish tinge of fluorescent or low energy lamps.

- ☹ Advertising which begins with the word 'Only' and continues with a sum of money which I am quite sure I will not be paying.

- ☹ Fast food in 'food courts' - places to go if you want industrial products-laced-with-appetite-boosters, extra sugar and salt, in a carbohydrate vehicle heated in a bath of low-cost oil.

- ☹ The stink of the last mentioned ingredient.

- ☹ Women with both hands full of fashion shopping bags loaded with new-purchases.

- ☹ Women, apparently lacking a guidance system, who wander across my path or stop suddenly,

- ☹ Tannoy messages in saccharin tone encouraging me to seize today's special offer.

- ☹ Having to negotiate multiple escalators which have been arranged so that you are obliged to walk past a maximum number of shops to a/de-scend to other levels.

- ☹ That the lavatories are in a remote location.

- ☹ That in many shop assistants are few and know little about the goods they sell.

I trust the above indicates clearly that I shop only when I must. My preferred alternative is to make or improvise a solution to my need, if I can. So wandering around one of Bristol's several cathedrals of capitalism wasn't fun.

That is until one day I saw a rather unusual exhibit featuring a police car, four police officers – one woman, two men, one canine, the latter with attractive patch markings and robust-looking teeth.

What I saw reminded me of those lotteries you come across at airport departure halls where a flash car - Porsche, Ferrari or similar could be yours if you're lucky.

The **Object** of **Desire** sits gleaming on a plinth together with a 'Don't touch' notice - 'Only 1000 tickets are being sold. Get one today. Somebody will be the proud owner in a few weeks' time. It could be you'.

Was the idea here was to raffle the brightly striped police vehicle, perhaps to fund the force's Christmas party. I asked about this; it did not amuse.

I turned my attention to the patched dog, his mix of ancestry producing, whether by chance or design, wonderful characteristics – imagine a human teenager, then think of the opposite - obedient, alert and competent.

The officer-in-charge was holding a ball in his hand, dog was lying flat, paws to the front, mouth open, tongue to the side, eyes fixed rigidly on this **O**-of-**D**. The officer continued to talk to the shoppers who had gathered around. Dog maintaining intense focus on fascinating object.

Officer makes as though he will throw ball; dog is familiar with this deception and remains unmoved.

Officer chucks ball; ball in dog's mouth in time's smallest increment. Dog makes happy whoofling noises. Policeman tells dog to release ball and is obeyed.

Policeman has dog moved away from car so dog doesn't see what comes next, then officer hides a packet of something within car engine bay (bonnet up). Dog brought back and told 'Find'. Dog on to car in millisecond, snuffling against area of concealment. Dog signals great job satisfaction with energetic tail action. Audience deeply impressed. Officer says, 'He can find anything'.

So good was this that after a round of the shops with partial success finding prezzies, I return for a second performance.

'You're a good dog', I congratulate the star.

* * *

Sheep, rain and Croeso

In my search for what could be my next home, one possibility I thought would suit was to live in an eco-community, so I researched. What quickly became evident is that the idea of joining one was not mine alone. I found a website with a listing of eco-coms; some way down the descriptions was an information field <accepting new members> and apart from one exception this was filled with the word 'No'.

Instead it read 'New members considered'; the location, rather-a-long-way-from-anywhere, Wales, but still closer than the Buddhist community in the Lake District I had also been thinking about.

There was a phone number, so I called and had a friendly chat with a woman. She asked me to write to them and I did, and then waited heap long time for a reply. When it finally came, the eco-people suggested a date for a visit. I passed the interval impatiently and expensively in Bristol and Birmingham hostels.

If you want to reach the eastern edge of mid-Wales, starting from Bristol, the fastest public transport is by train via Newport, but it's expensive. Cheaper is to take a low-cost bus service to Birmingham and complete the journey on a Welsh-bound train. This journey can't be done in one day if you want to arrive in the morning, so I stayed overnight in Birmingham and went for the train early the next day.

At least that was the plan.

I hiked a complicated route from the Central Backpacker's hostel to New Street station and there learned that the service I had planned for was cancelled, the next one to leave an hour later at 10:00. So then a text to inform eco person-with-car who was to collect me from Welshpool station.

Leaving Birmingham on a grey day, the view from the train was not inspiring, an ugly mix of industry, commerce, canal and dreary housing. Approaching Wales it improved, less of the former; more sheep. It was raining when I got off and walked over a winding bridge/path from platform to car park, where waited my picker-upper, a friendly woman, who was efficiently combining collecting me with buying supplies, there being no shops close to the eco-house.

Welshpool town although small, appeared to have all the essentials and I thought that the degree of isolation I would be facing could be withstood.

After a rather scary ride, since the country roads are narrow, bendy and everyone seems to go too fast, we arrived at the house. It's at the top of a steep drive which ends in a muddy patch between house, hen/geese quarters and the face of a cliff – if that's the word - it might be escarpment.

There were signs of building-work-in-progress, piles of roofing materials and drainage components. The main house's newly-slated roof looked well done, in rainy Wales a good thing. We stepped carefully down a slippery path, through a door and into the kitchen.

Seeing this gave me a good feeling, it's just the style that I like, functional-funky. There was a large wood stove in a corner, a couple of armchairs, a scrubbed wood table, pots hanging from a ceiling beam and warm lighting.

Introductions were made; I was shown my room for the next two nights – this guest accommodation being one of the fully finished parts; then I was toured around the rest of the house and surrounding land.

With a wheelbarrowful of bank notes and patient toil for a decade this could be made a very nice place. Shame about the Welsh climate.

The eco-peeps

The founders of the co-op, were a couple with teenager, another two unattached (possibly unattachable) women, and a beardy bloke. They seemed sorta-friendly. We chatted a while, ate something organic. Feeling the need for repose I ascended the very narrow staircase to my bedroom. The manoeuvre to accomplish this consisting of sideways-then-up actions more appropriate to crabs than humans.

At the top and around a corner was an attractively decorated room, wooden floorboards with rug, a small sofa and above it a platform bed. The carpentry was quality work, in one respect a bit too good; the timbers had been cut so precisely that the edges were sharp to the touch and climbing up the ladder and transiting to bed without pain required care.

I slept well and awoke pre-dawn next day. Since the lavatory was one staircase and multiple doors away, I relieved myself into a large and decorative jug, opened the window and added my contribution to the falling rain. A three month trip on a small sailing boat had cured me of conventional sensitivity; at sea bucket-and-chuck-it is standard practice.

When I judged it no longer too early, I descended to the kitchen below and had a go at re-starting the wood stove. I've developed good technique for this; the house in Germany has an ancient and partially kaput stove. By much experimentation I had found a way of getting it going even when there was little kindling and still damp logs.

The Fire Service terms the magic agent, accelerant - often mentioned in reports on arson. I used 'Brennspiritus' in DE; the British equivalent, 'Methylated Spirits', known commonly as 'Meths'. If you choose to try this ignition-booster, two suggestions: make sure your household building insurance is paid up; and hide the alcohol container where no one will be able to find it. Some mirror time getting your 'innocent' face as convincing as possible would be a good investment too.

There was none of this highly flammable aid to hand, but gentle raking in the ashes located a still glowing ember. Sustained blowing generated a flame; a few pieces of nearby dry wood did the rest. When the ladies of the house appeared a while later, I was asked 'Did you start the fire again?' The tone of voice indicating some disapproval.

The order of the day was breakfast; feed chickens and geese; make ready for delivery of pipes and fittings for new sewer line, prepare and eat lunch.

I wanted to show willing and lend a hand as appropriate. This never came to pass; I stood around looking rather useless until the lunch hour approached. At least then I could engage in some spud-peeling and veg chopping. I did rather too much of this in over-compensation so it was decided that I should cook the evening meal and use up the surplus. Here I was in comfortable territory, I like cooking and this household had a good stock of spices and other materials useful for making superior food. A veg curry was the end product.

Then followed a gathering of the eco-com members and a sort of tribunal to examine me for membership suitability. I thought it went off OK but it turned out a couple of days later that it hadn't.

Perhaps the court would have favoured me more if I had kept my responses short and to the point, instead of longer, with attempts at humour. Trying to be funny is a mistake most of the time, in most places, with most people. I knew this but couldn't suppress the urge.

If you aren't sure what I mean, just try British humour in the USA

At any event, the day I left, sitting on the Birmingham train I received a text with the news that I was a persona of insufficient grata. 'We don't think you would fit into our community.'

Oh well.

The jolly old ego did feel a touch bruised after this rejection, but rationalisation set in shortly. 'Probably best that I didn't join them, bit of a confined setting if feelings are not fully harmonious'.

Bastards.

* * *

Hope and hope-dashed

The morning of my departure from Tan-y-Fron I was watching the time closely. With multiple stages to the journey ahead, I was keen that nothing went awry. First, lift by car to Welshpool rail station, then train to Birmingham and with a bit of luck I catch a Snap bus (like Megabus, but cheaper) back to Bristol.

The start went to plan and I was dropped off at the station car park in rain and blustery wind. Then back over the elaborate, curvy footbridge to the platform. So much water was leaking from the sky that the shelter of basic 'bus stop' design was not performing its function well; I was becoming increasingly wet, ditto the one other would-be passenger.

The train's due time came . . . and went. A little Googling found that the service had been peremptorily cancelled, next train in an hour. So I invited wet-lady to accompany me to the station house to see if we could obtain refreshment – and more importantly, get out of the rain.

Wet-lady thought this a good idea and so over the bridge we went for a second time.

It's funny/strange how stations have changed over the last decades, what one might imagine to be the core use of such establishments, the provision of information and tickets-to-ride now largely replaced by knickknack shops and cafs of the expensive/pretentious/naff variety. Entry was through one such shop.

Given that Wales is a land of highish unemployment and lowish wages, the prices for drinks and snacks were surprisingly dear but accepted with mild-but-ignored protest since it was good to be out of the horrible weather.

Now-less-wet-lady and I chatted until the time came to return to the platform. Our transport turned up, on time too.

Boarded and seated, we talked more and my journey companion informed me that she was en route to visit her daughter in Cheltenham. Her usual residence near the Welsh coast was at Dolgellau – a name pronounced only marginally like what the spelling indicates to an English speaker. In the improbable event that you need to read this passage aloud, imagine that the place is called Doll-geth-lee.

* * *

The prospecting principle

At this stage of odyssey I was basing efforts to find my next home on something that was drummed into me by some years as a door-to-door salesman. What I learned then is that if what you are offering is something which definitely some people buy, then with persistence you can be sure that you will make a sale. The principle applies equally in many life circumstances.

I tell the lady sitting next to me what I am looking for. She will be about number 30 in my self–imposed exercise to ask one hundred people if they know of some form of accommodation which would be suitable for me.

And guess what, this lady is indeed one who does. She tells me that she and her husband live on a large property – land, historic-but-ruined-house, other buildings and another house that they actually live in.

There's a saga here; later I find out more by Googling the historic house. Related news items pop up too. The ancillary buildings used to be a school for children in care but it was closed some twenty years or so ago. This was connected in some manner to a scandal about mistreatment of children in 'special' schools. The buildings have been disused since.

This seemed like a possible fit for my requirements because not only did/do I want somewhere to lay my head, it would be ideal if there was also storage for my possessions. There are a lot of them, books, music, tools, furniture, memorabilia, family albums, and junk-which-is-too-good-to-dump; enough to fill a twenty foot shipping container, for sure.

The lady formerly-wet-but-now-drying-out said, 'Write to my husband'. And at the first opportunity I did but never received a reply. So I checked the address I had used, found an alternate and wrote to that. No reply from there either. Why I didn't hear back remains a mystery.

* * *

A strange way to return to Bristol

I had some interludes from the Bristol hostel existence and after one of them, returning from my son's place near Stuttgart, Germany I'd routed back to Bristol via Venice. Yes that sounds nuts I know, but having looked at all the alternatives, the cheap ones that is, it was the least bad option going, or rather, returning - if you see what I mean.

It must be around 15 years since I had last visited Venezia, so this irregular itinerary wasn't a bad thing; chance to see the old place, before it's gone, sunk in the smelly ooze.

There are several hostels on the main island but I booked the A&O in Mestre which is the last stretch of the mainland before the causeway to the Centro Storico, the main touristy part. Compared to those in the environs of many airports, the A&O hostel is conveniently located; airport to town by train for €2.00, then a few hundred yards walk to final destination - easy.

Emerging from the crowded train station, I took a couple of wrong directions where the path took turns to left and right, but within a few minutes could see a distinctive marker for the hostel - there are a half dozen sofa-like seating furnitures in bright colours set outside. They resemble cushy settees but aren't, being made of hard, ungiving plastic. The main purpose, apparent later, to provide an outdoor spot for smokers to practise their unpleasant practice.

In-checking went fast - I declined the optional bedding, for which this hostel chain charges extra. I had a thin sleeping bag liner with me for such eventuality, but I didn't need it since on my way up to the room spotted a housekeeping trolley with a pile of new sheets and covers. A quick shufty for security cameras - none that I could spot - so I helped myself. A crime, minor, but still an offence of some sort I expect, but to translate from a German phrase, 'No complaint: (so) no judge'.

With essential room activities accomplished I headed down to the common area, one of the A&O chain's signature vast halls, this one long enough for small planes to get airborne or sports day races. At one end the reception/bar hybrid, at the other several areas with seating, tables for computing and further on a considerable dining area. And in all this space, not a lot of people.

I went out for a bit looking for something to eat but without success, came back and sat at one of the well-appointed computing tables. These are big enough for three or four people on each side, with all the power sockets you might need and some fancy desk lamps. When I took up position only two others were there, one a fifty-ish man with greying, frizzy hair. The other a woman, (sorry no description available, use your imagination) - I took little notice of either but when the curly-topped gent was preparing to leave, I uttered something or other and a conversation began.

* * *

Crazy André

André, an American of Polish extraction, is an author, film producer, company-director and madman.

Some of the above could be substantiated with internet searches; Amazon does list one of his books. Other evidence supporting his tales takes the form of photos from his phone - from our beginnings to the point where I blocked further sendings, André would each day dump a slew of images on my WhatsUp account.

He starred in some of them, often in the company of attractive women but most of what he sent was mystical, new-agey motivational tosh. That was his big thing.

What he and his books are about is getting stuff; making things happen, through the power of inaction. This may strike you as counter-intuitive, it does me. André though, has certainty about its effectiveness. Think the right stuff, with consistent intensity of course, and the universe will do your bidding.

Hang on, there's a parallel here with the old believe-it-and-you'll-see-it religion pitch.

André wants a super-yacht, the sort that fill the harbours of the Cote d'Azure; lots of shiny plastic, polished metal, varnished wood - decorated with a well-appointed young woman or three. He's chosen a Princess 40M, 131 ft, not the most expensive super-craft by several kilos of gold, but still in the $30 to $60 mill bracket, depending on fit-out. It's not ostentatious or vulgar, simply a water-borne pad with room for a few guests. André has already had words with the builders about the options he'd like. He's materialising it for delivery next summer.

Meanwhile, he asked, 'Have you got a couple of Euros?' I gave him a ten E note and left, heading for bed.

Next day, André was already *à table* and computing, he broke off to chat with me. By this point I had let slip that I have written books, André wanted to know more. Very quickly the conversation moved to how he would 'amend' my book to suit his ideas and then get it promoted by a big-time American publisher. We would split the proceeds largely in my favour.

With hindsight, I should have been more insistent in checking his credentials –

'How well are your own books selling?'

André said he didn't know.

To me that is deeply suspicious, an author who doesn't know how well his books are doing. But at the time I rationalised that since my contribution to world literature was no longer making me any money at all, I had nothing to lose.

A. asked me to give him a copy of my principal book, saying he would add the touches needed for his audience. I consented and emailed him the doc.

One thing I will say in A's favour is that he is a focused worker. For the remainder of the day, he stayed at it. Progress reports were given to me periodically and by night he had completed the compounding work.
Here's an excerpt:

> *Your Mind is Your Only Limitation. Your conscious manifestation skills transfer from one industry to another and are the material you lace your resume with. Only your mind can limit you with the illusion of fear or doubt when it is time to make a move or change. At this point it is time for you to be conscious and be aware of the fear or doubt. Observe it. Let it go and take inspired action on a job or career change to achieve your targets. Make a decision to work on those which are within your circle of influence. And the most important of those is - You! Be conscious aware. Exit any self created traps your mind has created for you with the thoughts that it has generated.*

My immediate reaction to this wording was not favourable but since doing things my way wasn't working it would be wrong to dismiss André's approach without giving it a try - empiricism rules.

It wasn't easy to convince myself about this and I spent the next two days uncertain. What I didn't want was to lose credibility in my niche market - mostly engineers and scientists of the feet-firmly-on-the-ground variety. I couldn't see them lapping up new-agey verbiage.

André was ready with a contract which only needed a set of blanks filled and then signed. The deal was to be 25% to 75% split of revenues, him to me. I was happy enough with this since currently my 100 percent of no sales, was worse. He told me that he had another writer under contract but the advantage with me was that my book was already complete and could be offered to a publishing house without delay.

Following a reckoning as to what hour it would be in Santa Barbara, CA André made a phone call to the personal assistant of Jack, a man with ties to Mark Victor Hansen. I didn't obtain clarity as to how these two connected, but André spoke with reverence of Jack, and I was well aware of MVH and his big success, 'Chicken Soup for the Soul'.

'It's become a franchise', said André, meaning that the original 'for the Soul' has become 'Soup for any viable market segment you can dream up'.

One they may have overlooked perhaps, 'Chicken Soup for Chickens'.

MVH is now an A-lister in the publishing world hence unreachable by commoners, Jack would be our intermediary, but he too had enough celebrity to shelter behind a P.A. She is called Ruth and André had just tried phoning her. No good - voice mail. We tried later, no better. Then she called us back.

It was clearly California on the line, both accent and vocabulary making this evident.

I could sense that Ruth didn't know who André is, but she was being careful to accord him respectful treatment in case he was a big name that somehow she wasn't familiar with - very professional. The opening phrases were generic but friendly, we established that the weather on both continents was pleasant and that all parties were in good health. I was introduced; Ruth seemed impressed that I hail from London, giving me a measure of kudos from the get-go.

We got to the business of the business and Ruth asked with careful phrasing what we had in mind. Was it, for example to sign up for Jack's Writing Success workshop - maximum 12 people, price for the week $8,000?

André said that indeed he wanted to be part of that experience and would be sponsoring me for it too. Ruth gushed that it would be great for us to attend; she was impatient to meet and get to know us. So did André want to confirm the places with something she could take to the bank? Tricky, tricky, tricky - I was very interested to see how André would handle that one.

No problem, water off a waterfowl, André had a line ready to suit.

'That's exactly what I'm manifesting right now'.

'So you're going to manifest the workshop fee?' - Ruth.

'Sure Ruth.' We'll be back to you very soon'.

'That's great André'.

All well and good thus far but we hadn't got to what I would have thought was the main objective - would Jack/MVH be interested in parting with some serious cabbage for my/our book? Ruth too was edging around to 'Is there anything else on your mind?'

So André launched in with a word salad which needed lots of dressing - I was itching to take over and express our interest succinctly. André either couldn't or didn't want to.

Ruth gave me an opening,

'Rob, tell me a bit more about your book?'

I offered my standard elevator pitch.

'It's basic sales training for engineers and scientists. There is a big market in the US'.

Ruth understood this and said it was interesting.

The call had lasted nearly half an hour; Ruth had another meeting to get to. So we cut to the 'Great talking to yous' and 'Take cares'.

What that all had accomplished was not clear to me, an introduction had been made certainly, a first move on the chess board, met with a safe response from the other side, but as yet no sign of our master strategy. My doubts continued.

But you can't say that mystical new-agey stuff doesn't sell, it most certainly does. Not long after I was in Waterstone's bookshop, Bristol. I had gone in there only as a shortcut to another part of the shopping mall. In my way was a table on which lay books with such titles as - 'Your Universal Greatness'; 'Chakra Miracles'; 'Dare to be a Savant'; Crystal Living Vibrations'

So one could at least be certain that such works are being published, but more importantly do they sell?

I asked an assistant and he confirmed that customers are lapping the stuff up. Then he led me to a section of the store I hadn't noticed and there was an entire wall stocked with further variants, evidence in abundance.

In view of this confirmation that A's ideas were very much *de jour*, I forwarded a copy of the doc-as-modified-by-André to my engineer/scientist son Charlie, asking for his opinion. His reply settled the matter:

'It looks like André is trying to pack as many keywords into a sentence as possible. For Google Bots perhaps good, otherwise for the human reader it comes across as utter tripe.'

I forwarded this to André, he replied:

'Charlie operates at the level of his mind which is fine for him. I operate a bit differently.'

True that.

So was this the end? Far from it - for the next eight weeks there followed a deluge of WhatsUp messages, here's a sample:

> REMEMBERANCE=HUMILITY, ARROGANCE=LIFE IN THE ILLUSION OF DUALITY   (His all caps)

And:

> *The words are vibing and flowing off the Apple. Conscious Abundance - next global best seller. Push the money materialization energy my way. It materializes.*

I still couldn't dismiss André's approach completely. The idea that stuff 'materialises' just because you think about it obsessively is both right and wrong.

It doesn't matter how much mental effort you put in to hoping you win the lotto. In the absence of supernatural intervention, the laws of probability alone govern your chances.

On the other hand, obsessive focus on having or accomplishing just one thing enormously increases the odds in your favour. The mechanism is this: we humans are equipped with sensors which detect information of many types - you see, hear, smell, taste, touch things. Were you to log in detail every single input which occurs even in a short interval, the list would be long.

Here is what I am aware of in this instant. The amount of light in my room; a background hum from a refrigerator; the air temperature which is exactly right for me; the whiteness of the table surface my computer sits on; the residual taste of coffee in my mouth; the ease with which my fingers click the keys; a tightness in my stomach and a slight pain in my back - I need to get up and stretch - and so on. Pay me 25 cents an item and I'll list many more sensations.

As a thought experiment, let's say that there are always at least 100 sensory inputs entering your brain. What should you do with them, what makes the most sense, which are the most use to you?

Can we agree that if we accord equal value to all inputs, then it is likely to lead to a) overload and b) resources being applied to things which aren't very important while those that are get insufficient attention?

The good news is that the brain has a mechanism to do this; it triages incoming information, picking out the stuff which matters and ignoring that which has little value. That's rather convenient, but this function can be improved on - and it's here that André's ideas (not truly his of course, since the concept is ancient) make sense.

Decide what you want to have, do, be and post reminders where you will see them every day/hour/ and location and you will find that the desired thingy does indeed manifest/materialise provided no natural, human or scientific laws are being flouted.

A woman of 92 will never be a young beauty again, a Negro man will never be white, a dead person will never be brought back to life by the power of thought.

But if I want to find a pound coin lying on the ground somewhere or to meet a woman who speaks French and has red hair, or get a job as assistant to a billionaire, concentrated focus will increase my chances enormously. To do that, I need to be reminded to keep my attention on the desired outcome; become distracted, and the chance of success leaks away.

So with the mentioned caveats I do accept that enough visualise = materialise.

* * *

Wimmin
(Don't get upset with me for using this term, I refer you to Private Eye magazine, where there is a column with this title; complain to Ian Hislop, Editor.)

I haven't told you much about the women in 24 All Hallows. It's deceptive, at least to an innocent such as me; if you'd asked I would have said that they are all OK, unremarkable, normal (if you've come to accept that 'normal' embraces crazy).

Del knows otherwise; 'They're tarts the lot of them', he tells me one day.

'You know that one with the stick, I see her last night. She was walking along the road and a car pulled up and the geezer said, "I'll give you twenty pound for a blow job."

She opened the door, got in and done it'.

'That other one, in the room at the top of the stairs, she's on the game too. Her boyfriend is pimping her. I heard him say, 'Give me what you got'' and he took her money and a bottle of vodka too'.

It emerges that all the younger men in the hostel have had sex with Melanie, another of our crew. 'She wants 40 quid for it' Del says, 'I said naah to her. Not paying 40 quid for that'.

The slim and attractive-if-you-are-in-the-mood Somalian woman comments about another lady who, we're told asks for two hundred quid, 'That's an expensive prostitute'.

Del tells me – 'The Somalian one's on the game too'.

So if I'm not mistaken it's full house, every last woman in our residence is selling it. Hold on, the Portuguese lady has a job; she works in a kitchen at the airport. She'd be the one exception.

None of them has made me an offer though, I don't know why. Maybe I'm too old, in any case I wouldn't. At least that's what I say sober, pissed up might be a different matter.

But I don't want to; Del has told me, 'That one has an infection', I don't know which he is referring to, but even drunk hearing that would be enough to put me off. In any case I'm too tight - forty quid, naah man.

* * *

There is a middle-aged woman here who I often talk to. She comes over as pleasant but a bit lacking in normal adult skills – one day I suggested that she might cook some potatoes to go with the meal she was making. She replied, 'I don't know how to do that'. She mostly eats pizzas and (although the next remark puts me at risk of arrest by the PC police) has the body type which ensues.

Recently she brought one back from a local frozen food store. For her heating this up was a challenge; using an oven not easy.

I put all this down to perhaps an upbringing where everything was done for her and that may in part be true but today I learned of another factor.

Del had hinted at this some weeks ago but I hadn't fully grasped what he was saying; that's what happens when non-specific terms such as 'fing', 'geezer' and 'bird' make up much of a communication. I don't like to interrupt too often requesting clarity, so meaning is often unclear.

'I see loads of needles in her drawer' said Del. He also mentioned, 'She got some money out of her bag and there was dozens of condoms. She must be on the game, why else would she have so many?'

The new element I was told today was from J. who said, 'You see her up the road, waiting. She's waiting to get her drugs, she's on class As'.

I told J. that I am naïve, I never noticed anything to make me think she's an addict.

'When you've been doing the job as long as I have, you can see it', she replied.

Further to this, I was sitting in The Long Bar, Old Market, Bristol one early p.m. and a bloke recognised and hailed me. Unusual, unlike my German town where apparently everyone knew who I was and where I would be greeted within minutes of leaving my front door – in Bristol, a city with fifty times as many people, this had not yet happened.

The fellow in question was/is another resident of All Hallows, a fairly recent arrival; so far I had not got to know him, he knew my name though.

He told me what was worrying him, his bank card had been stolen - he now had a replacement but was still waiting for a new PIN code. Without it he couldn't withdraw any money.

These things happen; I've lost cards from now and then, but in his case there was a rather unsettling detail, as he explained.

Describing his dealings with the same lady-of-the-pizza just mentioned. 'She asked me if I wanted sex', he said. 'She's cock-happy'. 'I told her I wasn't interested'.

'Next time I looked for my bank card it was gone. She put sixty quid's worth of charges on it'.

From the upset tone in which he told this to me, I believed his account to be true. But you never know, this stratum of society is less constrained to morality of-the-middle-class variety.

Why she didn't offer her entertainment services to me, I don't know. If she had, I'd have declined politely. And my bank card wasn't at risk when in her company because I am very careful to hide it away until/unless I need to do some shopping. Nevertheless, that I had not picked up any clue to her criminal nature was a bit unsettling.

* * *

Tobacco, according to Del

'You know that geezer what discovered America', says Del.

'Raleigh, Del?' I suggest.

'Yeah, that's it, Raleigh. He went over there and the Indians said "Sit down with us and have a smoke". And they was smoking cannabis. Straight up that was what they was smoking'.

'Anyway he goes back to England and Queen Victoria asks him what he done over there and he tells her that the stuff is good, and he has a bit with 'im and she tries it'.

'Oh this is good' she says, 'Go back there and get some more, we can make a lot of money selling this'.

So he goes back to America and tells the Indians he wants a load of it, and they say

'Naah, we ain't giving you that to sell. When you was here we give you some of it as a welcome. We've got this other stuff you can have though'. 'It was tobacco man, not cannabis. That's why we're smoking tobacco now. The old queen was pissed off though'.

* * *

Del is (in)famous

Do leopards ever learn new tricks; do old dogs lose their spots? Do gangsters retire?

Twenty years ago, Derek and a pal acquired lotsa money, had a spot on TV and appeared a few weeks later at the Old Bailey (The top court for criminal offences in the UK). The formula or as Old Bill calls it, their modus operandi, was simple and very violent.

'We'd get suited and booted and go and wait in the big hotels, near the bank. Did you know some of them places have banks in the basement? We'd sit in the coffee shop, holding up the Financial Times and wait for some Arab geezer to go and draw out a load of cash.

We 'eard one of them say, "Seven thousand pounds please" so we followed him up to his floor and after he gone in his room we kicked in the door and said,

Open the safe or we'll shoot you'.

'We done this four times. They said we took one million pounds, my share was actually three hundred grand'.

We was on Crimewatch, with wossname, not the one what was murdered, the one who was on after, Fiona Bruce. We made a mistake, we stayed in our neighbourhood, Hackney, and one day a copper was walking past me and he stopped and said, "I know you". We should have gone away.'

I replied, 'Same thing happened to that gang which robbed the Kardashian woman in Paris'.

Del doesn't go in for the spectacular stuff anymore; he served six years 8 months of a ten stretch and prefers to stay out now. But there are hints that he's still doing a bit of work, but so petty you can hardly call it criminal. He asked me,

'What kind of meat you like, Rob?'

'Steak, Del'.

'I'll see if I can get some', he replied.

A few days later, he hands me a supermarket pack containing two sizeable pieces of rump. I offer money but he waves it away.

'How much was it Del?'

'That's alright, Rob, five-finger discount'.

Supermarkets lose a lot of meat, cheese too. Shortly after, outside the Chelsea Inn, I got talking to a rather smartly dressed fellow, smart for that neck of the woods at any rate. He asked me and the others nearby, 'Do you want some lamb chops?'

I asked a question which immediately seemed naive,

'Why are you selling it?'

'I stole it' came the frank reply.

He had a bottle of fine wine also, the price label said £12.

'Do you want it for a fiver?'

I declined, but regretted it later that evening.

A couple of years before I was staying in south London at a friend's place and one day he announced, 'We can do some roast lamb on Sunday'.

That's something I really enjoy but get to eat infrequently because of the cost. Since my friend Pedro had no visible means of support, I was surprised that he could afford such a pricey delicacy.

The mystery was solved that evening when the street intercom sounded and Pedro buzzed the caller up. He had a package with him - a leg of lamb. Pedro handed over ten pounds, about half what the price ticket said and both sides were happy.

'Addicts', Pedro explained. 'I tell them what I'm after and they go shopping for me.'

* * *

Love in the hostel life

At the risk of you thinking I am a dirty old man, I'll tell you that one thing I enjoy about staying in backpacker hostels is that you meet a lot of girls. Unfortunately the word 'girl' is where a problem lies. With the G appellation I'm referring to females of our specie aged from about 18 to 30. A simple calculation exposes that I am certainly old enough to be their dad if not his.

It's a rotten trick of nature, one of very few, to let old men fancy young girls. Biology establishes that vigorous young men and healthy young women make the best babies. Messing around with that simple principle increases the likelihood of unsatisfactory outcome in one way or another.

So why does big N make me feel sexual attraction to this inappropriate category? Over to you Desmond Morris (or Sir David if Des is busy). Let me know.

Morality, social conventions, laws are built on a foundation of long-accumulated experience, take the Golden Rule; to treat other people as you like to be treated. It makes for easy co-existence. (Unfortunately the familiar motto is flawed; suppose you prefer treatment which is different to what I enjoy? To obviate that ambiguity I suggest, 'Be nice'. It covers most applications and it's shorter.)

If I was The Creator (which is an irrational thing to say, since every living thing results from long time incremental modification, not a spectacular magic trick by a supernatural thingy), then at the age when coupling with a young woman starts to make for poor results, I'd suggest that male sex drive ought to fade to grey. To pick a number, let's say around age 45.

Full transparency: my own breeding record is outside of the limit just proposed. My oldest child was born when I was 41, but when my youngest hatched I was three years short of 50.

Now you are going to tell me that the Sir Mick Jaggers of this world initiate babies when others of their vintage are choosing cemetery plots.

If I was wealthy, healthy, famous and adored quite likely I'd be doing the same, regrettably I am a little short on four of those qualities.

In any case, what about the kids produced? What do they think when their friends' dads go down the park and kick a ball about and their own is sitting on the bench stroking his long grey beard?

Another thing; when you are old and decrepit and your wife is still fit and fanciable, can you really blame her if she plays around with another fella?

There are exceptions where the age difference doesn't spoil things, I know, but what the word exception means is that it is not the normal condition, it is un-usual.

Enough of this Phil O' Sophy talk, now, about the hostel girls I met and desired.

* * *

Julia What a wonderful fit she would have made as a girlfriend, warm, intelligent, a figure to make a judge wolf-whistle and she liked me. We had a great conversation - the topics I love to rant on. Then she said 'I wish I could talk about these sorts of things more often, I never seem to meet people like you'. I was primed to make her an offer, if I could sing I might have set it to music.

Elvis once did.

Wise men say only fools rush in
But I can't help falling in love with you
Shall I stay? Would it be a sin
If I can't help falling in love with you?
Like a river flows surely to the sea
Darling so it goes
Some things are meant to be
Take my hand, take my whole life too
For I can't help falling in love with you

The King is not alone in being impulsive, I'm guilty too.

Damn, damn, damn that it wasn't to be, couldn't be. She had a partner and I'd need extenuating reasons before stealing another guy's woman. And then the goddamn age gap thing again.

But she did give me a kiss when we parted.

This time I leave it to you reader, save me some typing and add to or rearrange the expletives which follow

$$\%\$@\#! \ \&^\wedge\$£ \ € \ \pm^\wedge\% \ ©β\$\%^\wedge{*} \ \&^\wedge\%\$$$

Thank you.

* * *

Yustina I was staying in the St. Christopher's Hostel, Bath a place of mediocre standard somewhat redeemed by the included 'free' breakfast. (Not really free of course, but if you subtract from the accommodation rate what that meal would cost elsewhere, you arrive at the cheapest place to spend a night this side of Cardiff.)

The St. C has no communal space for good contact between hostellers, the so-called 'chill out room' is horrible as I have mentioned elsewhere. So that leaves the dorms where you can begin the standard 'Where are you from . . . ?' dialogue, but there is usually a reason why your interlocutor will want to keep it brief - just arrived, making ready to go out and explore or the reverse, preparing to depart.

I'm curious and loquacious, so my need for a nattter builds up quick time. On this occasion, in the breakfast area, there were a couple of people at distant tables and one demure but attractive girl within easy chat range.

I used the standard opening, one that you will get heartily sick of if you travel in warmer countries, where it seems the further south you go, the more personal information will be requested and examined.

Beginning with 'Where are you from?' it continues with detail enquiries such as 'How many children you have?', 'What is your profession?' and so on.

These questions are not inherently bad, what is tiresome is that you find yourself answering them too often.

My reason for beginning a dialogue was one measure of the need for verbal exchange and one part the previously-declared-redundant opening move of courtship.

I am an old fool.

But you'd have to experience it yourself to appreciate what a lift I get when a pretty girl gives me a smile.

And that is what happened. Yustina, 31, gave me an open, somehow untarnished (I can't nail down exactly what I mean by that), friendly look and we began to talk. She was in England for the first time and just for a week. At home in Moscow she is a programmer, from the indication of intelligence that shone in her face, I wouldn't be surprised if she is also a skilled chess player.

We sat together for no more than 15 minutes when she announced that she had a train to catch. Her words on leaving, 'Now you have a friend in Moscow'.

This sentiment bitter sweet, since we had not exchanged contact information and outside of remote serendipity, it's not likely I will ever see her again.

For change this occasion cursing by **русский** language.

срать дерьмо́ блядь Сволочь Пиздец

* * *

Deborah is only a year or so shy of 50, but most of the time her behaviour and style have you thinking ten to fifteen years less. She's good fun, likes a drink and a laugh and can hold her own in a discussion. This may come from what she does as work; she's a specialist psychiatric nurse who deals with troubled teenagers.

She says she hates her job though and is about to return to studying to finish a PhD. That's not going to be easy financially because she will have to pay for the course herself. The money she's getting at the moment is good - temporary contracts through an agency. If she was careful with it, it would make future years without pay do-able, but she isn't. And while she was staying in a hostel when I met her, she chose a pricey single room and periodically when she needed more comfort she would treat herself to a few nights at one of the upmarket hotels. Add on a tenner or two for drinks each night and the weasel goes pop; that's the way the money goes.

I liked her from the outset, talking to her was comfortable; I could be myself, not in fear of PC transgression. She liked a joke and I fell into a sarcastic/ironic mode which approached the frontier of being rude, but I hoped never crossed it. At some point she asked me what I was looking for in a woman. I replied,

'One who's not expecting too much. You'd do'.

She laughed but I could tell that was a shade too near the mark.

We hung out a lot and saw numerous wine bottles come and go too. Partly these were supplied by Andrzej a man of non-specific Slavic origin. He must have had an easy source of money, since in the hostel a bottle of nothing-special red sets you back about £12 and one was never enough for him, more likely three in a session.

He had that characteristic of men from Europe's eastern edge, bibulous over-generosity. Those around him of an evening were prompted to get a glass and sit down with us.

Don't think I didn't exploit this even though such behaviour is shabby.

My benefactor reminded me of another Slav, that one from Serbia, a work colleague of long ago. He did the same thing with booze, money and miscellaneous other services. In the case of this Stefan, I eventually came to view the hail-fellow-well-met outer shell to conceal an egotistical, manipulative core. He was all charm and elegance with strangers and cruel to his wife. Once I had a fix on that, I dropped him.

Andrzej would intersperse other chat with account of his sexual adventures. Since we were in a hostel, one where most people will be sleeping in dorms, Deborah asked him where the action had taken place. There was slight hesitation before Andrzej replied; for Deborah a suspiciously long interlude.

'You didn't do it in the elevator?'

Andrzej indicated that this was correct, he hadn't.

'So was it in the bathrooms? Ugh that's horrible'.

When we were alone, Deborah asked my thoughts about this.

'He's just boasting. It's all fantasy', I said.

I really thought that she and I were a good match and I said so openly. The response wasn't the endorsement I would have liked, more non-committal. So in a moment of bravado, I thought,

'What the hell, what have I got to lose?' So I suggested, 'Let's go up to your room and have sex'. She didn't protest but she didn't agree to it either.

I didn't mind since I knew that I had done the right thing - I'd given it a try and that would be one less wasted opportunity for me to regret in my dotage.

The end of the affair was unsatisfactory; Deborah's contract was taking her to Birmingham next. 'I'll be coming back here before too long though'. And apparently she did return because another hosteller told me, 'I saw her on a bus a while back'. But I didn't and the texting stopped after a couple of rounds.

Boohoo, coulda, mighta worked out but didn't.

* * *

Fish and chip woman This episode has no direct connection with *la vie en hostel*, but it sticks in my memory as another case of instantaneous attraction.

Since I was still new to Bristol, I would often walk into areas I was unfamiliar with just to see what was there. In this instance the location was Denmark Street, which links the College Green area with The Centre. The side exit of the Hippodrome theatre opens into it, which is why a caf' there offers pre and post theatre dining. It also attracts a midday crowd to its fish-and-other-fried-stuff offerings.

When I spotted the place, it was well past normal lunch time and I was hungry. I went in and a pleasant waitress directed me to a room at the back; 'There's more space'.

(In hindsight I suspect that remark was referencing my corpulence and likely inability to fit into the front room's banquettes).

On the walls were posters from across multiple decades with the names of shows and performers, famous to obscure. For theatricals, the location was perfect, just across the road from their place of work.

'Have you decided?' asked the waitress and I responded 'Fish, chips, tea please'.

That short exchange was long enough for me to take in the very-much-to-my-taste, appearance of this 30-something woman.

I consumed the food, drank the tea, studied the posters then made ready to leave. As I was lining up to pay, the waitress looked and me and smiled. And that did it. On impulse I said to her, 'I like you. Can I invite you out?'

'I don't think my husband would approve' she replied with an amused but far from hostile look.

A man in a wheelchair, who I had not been aware of previously, turned around and said, 'Get your own woman'. My riposte was spontaneous, frank but not very clever,

'That's what I'm trying to do'.

I haven't been back.

You can get tired of this human merry-go-round.

*   *   *

Alpha nights

There's another episode before my 007 stay comes to its full and final stop and the engines have been switched off (oops that's Ryanair, sorry); the Alpha Course nights.

I was in what I think of as the centre of town, the top of Corn Street, the junction with Wine and Broad Streets. Here you find food stalls, the St. Nick's Market and nearby, 'Wetherspoon's The Commercial Rooms.

A deceptively fine rain was falling. You wouldn't write a song about it; it would need to be harder, (Thank you Bob), still I was getting wet. Light and hubbub was coming out of a nearby and ancient doorway - the entrance to the church which gives its name to the market. Having crashed more than a few gates in my life - and mostly gotten away with it - I approached and in the absence of bouncer slid in.

'Hello, have you been here before? Good to see you.' This from two young women, friendly and attractive. 'Come over here and we'll fill out a form. We're not starting for another few minutes.' That information scored low on relevance for me, considerably more interesting was being in the dry and in sight of food. The good wives of the parish were loading up a table with elements for a buffet meal of substance and variety. Was this, despite persistent doubt that it actually exists, the fabled Free Lunch?

On that day I was far from blasé about eating without charge; a quarter year later, I pay for food only when I'm too lazy to go and dine for no money. Sceptical? Then visit Bristol, there's more free eating here than you've had hot dinners.

Grub-for-the-taking deserves a chapter to itself; so far I have noshed gratis (or at token price) at four establishments and scored sandwiches and lunch bags at two more. As it happens I think I'll go try another down-and-out magnet this very noontime.

But back to St. Nick's; they aren't asking for money in exchange for what you eat, you 'pay' another way.

The organisers of this Alpha Course - *'A series of interactive sessions that freely explore the basics of the Christian faith. No pressure. No follow up. No charge'* -

aren't after your money, in exchange for a plate of food they want your soul.

I'm not new to this though, having once been caught up in another religious, or rather cult, recruitment trap; that one by the Moonies. Although it was long ago on another continent I have a good idea how this evening will play out.

These are the indicators:
- 'bait' girls approach you (if you are a guy) and chat you up
- there's an offer of food; 'But first a word from our leader'
- then testimonials from recent converts

- after which a movie featuring impressive landscapes and a motivational talk from an American 'pastor'
- a bit of praying
- followed by separation into small groups where a 'trusty' (a true believer) fakes a discussion with you - in reality, making an assessment as to whether you are convert material
- to finish, a sales pitch by the evening's Führer soliciting your longer term involvement. Tonight this is Toby, he looks sensible, intelligent but he's talking the talk of a true-believer. Three qualities which are more common in cynically manipulating cults than in nature.

The event aims to appeal to people of student age. There are testimonials from two young ladies, followed by lengthy religio-singing with two guitars. Clearly home-spun stuff, not a pop cover. The melody is unremarkable, the words unhip, clumsy, repetitive. Later they provide a basis for some complaining by me.

The lyric has a lot of, 'He is wonderful and great, let's praise Him, His love is wide, wide, wide and deep, deep, deep' (with hand gestures for emphasis). Then there's a minute or so of generic hymn-type wordage, followed by more wide-armed emphasis of His width and depth.

In case we haven't got the message, this 15 minute epic concludes with a last, final and ultimate suggestion that we should be telling Him that he is really a terrific guy.

Hang on, this isn't a Trump rally is it?

American satirists of Democratic leaning and psychiatric professionals repeatedly point out that Donald Trump in craving attention and praise is displaying symptoms of narcissistic personality disorder.

I put it to our 'discussion' group that the message of the song just performed is that believers should be offering up loads of the same to J-man. Which makes one question whether Jay's personality, credentials and motives are any better than those of Earth's (currently - 2019) most powerful man.

Maybe you haven't been to an induction session for one of those multi-level sales jobs for such companies as Amway, Herbalife, or Avon Cosmetics. I've gone to many - being a sucker for an 'easy-money' pitch.

If you had, you'd know that much of the belief-transfer is by means of people, selected to be similar to you, coming up on stage to tell you, 'I was unsure at first, but my friend got me to come along and I joined up. That was three months ago. My pay last month was $X,000 and I'm loving it'. This repeated with minor variation by several people.

The purpose is to both assuage your doubts and stimulate your desire for the big cheque. The formula is well-proven; similar approaches work in advertising and politics too.

Adapted for this outfit's recruitment drive, the testimonials followed this pattern: 'My life wasn't going well, too many worries, I was feeling bad and didn't know what to do.

Then my friend told me about Jesus-The-Fixit-Guy. All I had to do was tell him my troubles and he got everything sorted. It's great, now I hand anything tricky off to Lord J and he deals with it for me'.

What's not to like? If you can manage to avoid critical thinking, I can't see any reason not to go for the message - 'Your problems fixed, no credit card needed, no charge'.

The idea of walking out is never far from my mind, but two things are holding me back. I'd like to have some of the free grub, and one of the birds who chatted me up at the start said she would like to hear more of my story because she works for the BBC and maybe they could use my story, 'We're doing a piece about homelessness in Bristol'.

Finally we get to the group discussion phase. Aside from the 'trusty', there are five of us, including two women. It's clear that we are selected as old; off to one side is a much larger group of twenty-somethings. I don't like this division since I'm looking for an opportunity to denounce this culty brainwashing of young minds.

To my surprise, I'm not the only one with misgivings about what this organisation is really up to; there's a forty-ish Caribbean lady in our group and she gets a sharp word in first. I back her up with my opinion that religion does humanity far more bad than good.

Unsurprisingly the believers want to cite examples of the worthwhile stuff delivered by their supernatural benefactor. I counter this with, 'Do you think that religion brings people together or does it divide them? How many wars have been caused by religion?'

The faithful don't have much of a riposte to this but there's little sign that their trust in the god-pitch has taken a knock either.

The Gruppenführer now informs that next week we can enjoy some more of this in part two - 'Evidence that the message is true'. And at last the announcement I have been waiting for, 'Come and get some food'.

No complaints from me about that offer; salad, pie, pate, dips, quiche and desserts. But is it worth going through 90 minutes of mind-laundering another time? No not really, I'm not coming back. Or so I thought.

* * *

If I had kept my big mouth shut, this wouldn't have happened - Kev asks 'Had a good night Rob?' when I get back to the hostel. I could have headed this question off with a light platitude, but I didn't, I gave an account in some detail of the Alpha do.

Kev was intrigued; he particularly liked my rendering of the song-with-gestures part. I couldn't remember the exact words, but the bits which did the trick for Kev were the 'His love is wide, wide, wide and deep X 3'

'Go on Rob, do it again'.

Kev was fascinated, but more was to come; I told him about the testimonial offerings and how Jesus was taking care of the problems which had troubled these witnesses.

The idea is attractive; a party who will deal with the stuff you don't enjoy. Pretty handy. Take the household chores for example; ask nicely and maybe J-man will do the dishes for you.

Kev and I batted this idea to and fro for a considerable while; 'Do you think that Jesus could get my computer working again?'

'It's worth a try Kev, doesn't cost anything'.

Kev was sold, 'Are we going again next week?'

'I don't know if I can, there are some other things I might have to do'.

That was no good as an excuse, Kev brushed it aside immediately. 'No come on, let's go, we can ask difficult questions and have a laugh'.

Kev had home team advantage with the tricky questions for priests and their groupies - he had been adopted when young and was very sensitive about the well-being of children. He raged on the subject of holy perverts. The Alpha set up beckoned as a platform for him to get his demons out of the cupboard and do them some violence.

'If one of them touched my nephew, I'd floor him' - and I'm sure that Kevin would.

* * *

A week goes by and we reprise the Jesus-as-housekeeper concept often. Some research also gets done by me on the

Difficult Questions. I know a very good source for these, Christopher Hitchens's book, 'God Is Not Great – How Religion Poisons Everything' and I get it out of the library.

Tuesday evening comes and Kevin and I catch the 75 bus into town. At the church, Kev is disconcerted when he gets pulled aside and told that a form with his details is to be filled in. 'What do they want that for?' he asks me later.

He also reprimands me for leaving him on his own.
'I thought I'd give you a chance to chat up the birds Kev', I tell him.

Actually it was more that I wanted to get to the food - for these sessions, they feed you before all the preachy stuff.

Kev isn't very satisfied with my excuse, but he lets it pass since he wants to get to the grub too. What's on offer isn't familiar to him, 'What is this stuff?'

'Couscous Kev'. 'Ain't they got anything else?

He settles for just the sauce, minus c-c- and we move over to the area our group is to occupy. Disappointingly, there are only four of us tonight; three appear to have dropped out already. The trusty true-believer is there of course.

The program gets going, not much different to the time before. The music break is the same as I had told Kev about; he loves the 'wide and deep' bit and stands there mesmerised.

For unclear reason I behave in a way which is entirely out of character; I sway to the rhythm. It could be that it's my body speaking its language - communicating without words resistance to the solemn attention being offered by the rest of the crowd.

An idea is forming and will develop further before the following week's session; it's going to take insubordination a step further: nobody has applauded at the conclusion of the singing. The performance wasn't enthralling, but it wasn't pants either, polite clapping would suit, hooting and ululation not required.

I'm suspecting that all it would take to switch this around would be for one vigorous clapper to break the spell freezing the other spectators.

Kev agrees that we should do this and so one week later, as the last note of the song fades, Kev and I get going with hearty applause and just as anticipated, following a tiny delay 200 other hands are in noisy collision.

Chuffed we are with our success. On leaving, Kev, who isn't a big drinker, surprisingly suggests that we go for a pint. Wetherspoons is close by and we head there. Again with ulterior motive, I buy the beer - Kev says 'I'll get the next one' and he doesn't. Typical. Then back to the grotty hostel, a reprise or two of the night's best bits, and to bed.

In the days which follow, we chew over points raised in the small-group-of-oldies discussion session. There was one member who has told us how he 'came to the Lord'. He had an accident, I'm guessing it was on a motorbike, and it resulted in him losing a foot. The pain this caused was extreme; he was at the limit of his ability to bear it and beginning to wish that he could die. A priest (or some other variety of religion-salesperson) told him that Jesus did pain relief as well as general troubleshooting and Dan gave it a go. He told us that it worked, so he has kept up his subscription, the doubts he had about religion in his student days invalid now that he had experienced a bit of quality work from J-man.

Kev dismissed this, 'He would never be talking like that if he hadn't had his accident'. My thought too.

Kev and I improvised a double act for the so-called discussion sessions; when he got the chance, my associate opened up on the theme of pervert priests. I backed him up; when Kev's debating thrusts lacked oomph I interjected a smart (borrowed from Hitchens) line.

I'd judge that we won the argument if not by a knockout then at least on points. I mean what could they say – all those Catholic priests touching up and buggering choirboys, it had been all over the papers – no further argument, case closed.

All the believers could offer was, 'You can't condemn all priests just because some of them are bad'. Oh yes we can; they are supposed to be celibate - no sex, so what happens, they adapt to not having a wife as bed partner by queering little boys – bastards.

Kev maxed out on indignation at this and gave vivid description as to what he would do to one of the evil specimens should need or opportunity arise. He left us in no doubt.

There was another line of attack that I worked; why all the 'Praise him, for he is great' stuff? It's a frequent motif of religio-talk. I suggest to the members of our group that this is clearly narcissistic. 'What about the meek inheriting the earth'? Shouldn't He be setting an example?

I mean currently the most powerful man in the world goes in for volumes of self-praise and this is rejected and ridiculed by the majority of observers. So how come J-man is granted all the sycophantic flattery?

The event over, our route to the bus stop took us down Broad Street, which isn't very. You get a clue as to what kind of business is mostly transacted around there from office signage advertising an unhealthy number of legal outfits. What attracts them to this place is profitable work at the Bristol Crown Court. The main entrance is on a parallel street; we were walking past the back door, familiar territory to Kev,

'That's where I've got to go next week'.

If you are there of a morning, you'll see a number of smartly-suited but dodgy characters waiting around outside, most likely having a fag, sometimes they're sitting in a nice motor. They'd be the lead character's supporters I'd assume.

Kev makes a suggestion, 'We could go there and watch the trials, it's interesting'. That's probably true, but not really what I'm into, so I fudge a reply.

* * *

Kev lets me down

You know something about Kevin by now; he is the Mr. Mop of the double 0 seven hostel. His duties there, working for the Greek owner family are; moving floor dirt from one location to another with said floor maintenance tool; arranging and plumping up the sofa cushions; drawing the curtains shut after dark, opening them again next morning; and once a week changing the residents' bedding.

All this can keep him busy for several hours a week; how to fill the remainder? Texting to girls he's met accounts for a decent chunk; going down the road for a takeaway uses up most of what's left, and he's usually got the time to chat.

He tells me about his early life; he was adopted as a child by the couple who own this place. He doesn't speak Greek, but understands some of it, since it surrounded him when small.

The other children of the family are distinctive in their individual ways. The son, James has been handed day-to-day management of the hostel and in the period I had dealings with him was a right see-you-next-Tuesday; the daughter, Shazelia is occupied mostly with health irregularities and her children.

Review comments on hostel web portals inform you that many visitors detect something of a Cosa Nostra atmosphere in the double 0 seven. There is a background hum of threat in the place, despite the frequent sight of long term residents dozing on the sofa. Kev's talk of violence towards those who displease him and his current status of waiting for sentencing contribute to this.

What distinguishes Kev, and others I later came to know in All Hallows, is that they are largely free of the middle class' fear and loathing of prison and the dishonour which accompanies; consequently they are less restrained in their behaviour.

At the time I was staying at the 007 because it was the cheapest in town and permitted long stays (most backpacker hostels limit you to a maximum of two weeks). I was paying for the rent myself; later I would be granted Housing Benefit which helped towards the cost although it didn't cover it in full. For these two reasons I felt somewhat trapped and even though I disliked the hostel and management, I had no better plan.

Elsewhere I have listed the place' general deficiencies; worse than those were my sleeping conditions. I was in a room about 4m by 3m in which there were two double bunk beds – accommodation for four people. Beyond this space was a bathroom. It was used by all eight occupants of the rooms on this the first floor. To reach the bathroom, it was necessary to transit from the hallway through the space I slept in. Throughout the night there was traffic and the consequent noise of bathroom use.

You may think this unpleasant; it was. Even worse was the noise from the single other occupant of the passage I was sleeping in. He is/was an African of apparently imperfect health who snored loudly for much of the night. Somehow I managed to ignore this initially. At the time I had other worries deriving from my multiple health defects. Morning and night I had to inject myself in the stomach with a blood-thinning agent. This was less fun than you may think. Eventually I arrived at a technique which reduced the pain; slow insertion of the needle and extra-slow depression of the hypodermic plunger. Then it stung only a little.

The snoring-plus-snorting of my room neighbour really bugged me and as mentioned elsewhere I had no effective way to counter it. I tried lightly kicking his bed, or rattling the metal parts of the frame; I shone my über-bright torch at him; I went to the bathroom and slammed the door. Nothing was effective; I knew that in advance that it wouldn't be.

It would be fair to ask why I didn't just talk to him and make the problem clear. Perfectly reasonable to wonder about that; the why is that I'd tried doing so with other offenders and know that it's no use.

In the Bath St. Christopher's with a sizeable bloke, in a bed no more than one meter distant, who was practising zoo noise impressions. I poked him lightly and told him that he was keeping the whole dorm awake. My message angered him and he said,

'You touch me again and I'll belt you', adding, 'I can't help it, it's involuntary'' which of course it is.

In the 007 I somehow withstood six weeks of this nightly torture and during that time I complained to anyone who would listen, including Kevin. I also asked if there was a single room going which I could have.

'No'; even the staff members were sharing rooms – 'the owners gotta do it to maximize revenues'.

Then one night - perhaps I was drunk - I flipped and gave the snorer's bed a serious shaking while I shouted the obvious instruction to him, which amounted to 'Cease and desist, you who was born out of wedlock'.

Becoming conscious for a moment, he seemed surprised – that's the beauty of the offender's side of this matter; not having suffered the aural torment, appreciation of the nuisance is indirect.

In any case, words might not have been a good medium for communication; when I had heard this individual speaking on his phone it was in a lingo from the Dark Continent, other than that he had little conversation with staff or residents.

A day or so later Kev said to me, 'The African has been complaining about you'. I put my side of the matter to him. Kev replied, 'If it happens again, just call me; I'll sort it out'.

And of course it did, so I followed Kevin's suggestion and phoned him. The reply was disappointing, 'It's late Rob, I can't come round now'.

'But Kevin you said . . . ' Pointless, he hung up.

That was the pivotal moment and with it the realisation; 'Whatever comes next I am not staying here one more hour'. I switched on the light and packed my bags.

This is something to do with care since in hostel conditions items are easily lost and left behind and I was not planning on returning. Ever.

Twenty minutes of packing and checking under/in/and around the bed for things which could have wandered off during my stay and I was ready to depart. It was coming up for two am on a cold January morning.

With nothing definite in mind I intended to head for the town centre - the 007 lies a mile or so out to the south.

Since there is a bus stop not far, I went there and sat down to think about my next move and while that was not happening along came a number 76 and I got on. That part was easy and a great relief; so good to be putting distance between me and that awful place, but where to spend the next hours?

I was not clear about that. I could rule out a couple of the places I knew - The Old Port House - too horrible, the YHA too dear. Anyway the night was half gone; I didn't want to pay good money for the remaining hours.

Another of the town centre hostels is the St Stephen's Street Backpackers. I had never fancied it, just from the look of the outside; it's drab and neglected and in a street absent of any charm. A contingent of smokers – I'm not saying what they are burning – hang around the door most hours.

In the event, this was a good thing. I wandered up to the entrance with backpack and trailed suitcase and one of the aforementioned bods pulled open the door for me.

This was good, since no reception person is present through the night and with a selection of sofas to snooze on; I installed myself on one and did my best to sleep. Given the nervous energy expended in the previous hours that wasn't easy, but doze I did and the night slowly gave way to that which always follows even at the worst of times.

For me the 007 and Kevin were finished; he called me a couple of times, still anxious to continue with the Alpha Course at St Nicholas' church. But no, Kev, whether or not he could comprehend the significance of 'keeping your word', had overstepped a boundary and there would be no reprieve.

* * *

Language

Orright

Spend a day in Bristol and you are going to hear a bunch of 'Orrights', it is the people's standard greeting in these parts.

There are many ways to accost, speak to, salute, address, hail, recognise, embrace, acknowledge, bow to, approach, give one's love, hold on the hand, extend the right of friendship, hail, bid good day, bid hello, bid welcome, exchange greetings, move to, and usher a fellow human.

Not to mention the standard stuff of course, the 'goods' – morning/day/evening/night. Myself I favour 'Howdy Doody'.

And I think most of us are familiar with the Antipodean word-mangle, 'G'day' - and if you are prepared to tolerate that, I'll address you in French with 'B'jour', and the Teutonic, 'G'Tag'.

'No worries' is another product of the Southern Hemisphere which has infected Brizzle. Ugh! Hostel staff, barmen and for all I know County Court judges employ it.

Humankind disappoints me.

Now you are thinking, 'Omigawd what a pedant' and you may be right, but at least I do try to be a pleasant pedant.

Usually the point of asking a question is that you would like to know something - am I right? So what's with this 'Orright' business, asking a question but not waiting for or even expecting an answer?

If I enquire, 'Do your feet hurt?' or 'One lump or two?' and don't get an answer, I'll probably rephrase and try again; 'Still got the old leg-end trouble?'; 'Two sugars, or are you sweet enough?'

But although 'Orright?' is articulated question-style, its practitioners are perfectly happy if you bounce the same back to them without hesitation, repetition or deviation. It's a simple 'call and response' format: 'Orright?' : 'Orright'.

Simple, but difficult for this new arrival to tolerate, let alone adopt. Now after nearly a year around here I sometimes manage to resist answering this non-question with a short overview of my state of health, but not always.

'Orright Rob?'

'Thanks for asking. It's the knees and ankles mostly, chest's OK now. The doctor's put me on ....'

They don't want this, the full medical report; it's just a greeting fergawdsake.

Orright?

* * *

Yeah-uh

This is largely Del's fault. I love his style and vocals - that low-register Cockney resonates through walls and ceilings. There's an aspect of his sound art I find catching; I'll do my best to describe what I mean in words.

Bit stupid trying to explain sounds with words, of course - you might as well tell a blind man what a traffic light looks like or describe Mozart to a pussy cat.

Anyway.

The English-speaking people's principal affirmative is 'Yes' and it's good enough for around one point five billion Earthlings. When it comes to indicating enthusiastic acceptance or endorsement, speakers of the dialect Cockney employ a variant of their own. They stop the glottal.

'Yeah-uh we stop our glot-ulls'.

'Wossa glottal?' you ask. Answer, it's a small pause between the front and back ends of a word.

Perhaps you'd enjoy a more complicated answer:

The glottal stop or glottal plosive is a type of consonantal sound used in many spoken languages, produced by obstructing airflow in the vocal tract or, more precisely, the glottis.

Try it, you might like it. Have a go with the simple negative, 'no'. Inserting a G-S it becomes 'No-wuh' - now you got emphasis man.

'Lend us a coupla-quid'. To indicate that you would prefer not to, go 'No-wuh'. That should make it clear.

'Wanna drink?' - as your pal moves bar-wards, 'Yeh-uh' leaves no doubt.

Yeahman

To blend in to the Bristol scene one more element helps, 'Yeahman'. Mostly it's the yoof and the Caribbeans who employ this to signify agreement. It's catching I find myself saying it now and then.

While we are discussing langwidge here's another item I find hard to ignore.

Fings

'Don't touch the fing' says Dee, who does the housework in 24 All Hallows; her full name is Denise, 'But everybody calls me Dee'.

'What fing?' I ask.

She indicates an oven grill tray which is now lying on the sink draining board.

'I put that stuff on it, so don't touch it.'

'You put some of that stuff on the fing?' I ask.

'Yes, what's it called? You know, you mustn't get it on your hands.'

'Oh I see what you mean now; you've put some of the stuff on the fing what's lying on the fing'.

'Oven-cleaner, that's it. I couldn't fink of it at first'.

'Yes, Dee. I know that stuff; it's nasty'.

I shouldn't tease her, but she doesn't take offence, surprisingly quite the reverse, 'You're in a good mood today'.

It may appear so, but my head is still more than slightly foxed from last night's excesses. I don't tell Dee this because house rules – and I have signed a copy saying that I have read, and agree to abide by them - prohibit fire water of any type on the premises.

Oh dear, my bad.

Tomorrow's lesson: 'Ow to drop your haitches'.

* * *

Why Spaniards pronounce the letter V as though it is a B

This is à propos of nothing, other than that you hear a lot of Spanish spoken in Bristol. It's just an Interesting Fact -
(That's an echo of a Pete and Dud sketch, sorry Millennials, you won't have a clue what I'm referring to).

If you've been there or learned a little of the language you will know that in Spain there is no significant distinction made between how the letters B and V are pronounced, ¿*Vale?*

That last word is useful, in Spanish it does the same duty as *'Right?'* in Britspeak. What's weird about it for us is how the word is pronounced, it's like 'Bar lay' (imagine the well-known bank not having the letter c in the middle of its name.)

This V=B swap takes a bit of getting used to, so for example, Valencia isn't. It's Balencia when you are in that region. Vino isn't either, it's beano. Tricky eh?

How this has come about, I haven't yet researched; I might one day when nothing else presses. There's probably a pukka linguistics term for what's going on. In the same way that in closely related languages, you get a shift in spelling, example, the rodent is spelled Maus in German and pronounced exactly the same as its British cousin. Same goes for Haus, where again our British forbears kept the sound but changed the spelling.

I'd study this all if I got another long chunk of living – it appears that science will have us lasting until 150 in another couple of generations. - Just missed out on that, but on the other hand, I'm weary so my last dozen turns around the sun will do me.

But back to the Iberian puzzle, why are Vs Bs – and here I have an insight which someone in academia could work up into a thesis perhaps.

The answer is right in front of me, on my keyboard; the slightest error, a slip of the finger, one key confused with its neighbour and you have swapped the two. If there's not a qwerty layout in front of you at this instant, this is what the bottom row of a standard keyboard looks like.

$$\backslash\, z\, x\, c\, v\, b\, n\, m\, ,\, .\, /$$

Got it now?

More difficulties with language

I've mentioned a Kev or two in this account, one of them spoke fluent bad English – that's not *moi* being snobbish either, *non*, Kev, a plain speaker, says so himself.

Once on a holiday, I, two of my children and Kev's troupe were in a car near Venice, Italy. We were looking for a market. A likely looking signora was standing on the pavement within hailing distance, so I ventured a phrase in local lingo.

'Where is the mercado please signora?'

She gave directions and we set off following them.

Kev said something about my wonderful ability in spaghetti-speak, adding for emphasis, 'I carn eevn tork inglish'.

Of course he actually can but it's the dialect of his local clan, not quite the way the Queen speaks.

One hot summer afternoon Kevin invited me to his home to enjoy a splash in his pool. It's one of those plastic jobs, which look like they probably aren't going to last for very long, but they're not too dear and you can pack them away for the winter.

Because of the restricted dimensions, rather than swim, all one can do is bob about a bit, but that's good enough if your main interest is cooling off. We float and refresh. Diving is out, there is a warning against it. Kevin looks at the notice and asks, 'Ere Rob, wossat, knee paz plonger?' and I tell him.

Now supposing you woz from a different country and English still more an ambition than a present reality, wandering around a shopping area you see '*spudulike*'. What are you going to understand that to mean?

Google doesn't help with this as much as you might expect, the results I found lead in unlikely directions:

Do you mean spadelike? More suggestions:
spiderlike, spitlike, spoutlike, spurlike, spotlike, spurdike, souplike, podlike, spuddle, seedlike, sparlike, suitlike, spur dike.

Result; one confused foreigner.

So it is to be hoped that s/he does not encounter the next high street puzzler; *'pretamanger'*. I'll help you with that one – *'manger'* is most likely just a misprint for 'monger', you know like 'ironmonger'- supplier of ironware.

So logically this gives us, *'pretamanger'* - supplier of *pretas*.

Wossa *'preta'*? The dictionary says;

Preta (Sanskrit), Standard Tibetan, also known as hungry ghost – a supernatural being undergoing suffering greater than that of humans'.

Putting that together, we now have 'pretamanger' - a supplier of exceptionally hungry ghosts.

Glad we have cleared that up.

* * *

Before we leave the topic of English as it is spoke, there is one essential word I have not yet shared with you – a term which demonstrates that you belong, you fit in with the Bristol demographic, you are one with them.

It is: 'Rizla'.

Buy a pack of these meagre but highly valued cigarette papers - irrelevant if you smoke or don't - and you have *entrée* to popular society. It matters not if you want to be one of them; you may even consider them repulsive oiks. But say, for example, you need their vote because you are a politician with ambition for high office, then be prepared.

'Gotta Rizla please mate?' 'Certainly, take two'.

Or in particular Bristol neighbourhoods, 'Would three be more useful?'

* * *

Bad teeth

Are you aware that Americans think the British have bad teeth? No? Well that's their standard opinion. Funny, since they aren't too bothered about other aspects of appearance.

I mean the USA is a land where no one need feel under-dressed; go supermarket shopping in beachwear or a night robe and nobody stares; weigh 300 pounds and you melt into the universally obese background. But your gnashers must be pearly.

Not very natural though, given the abundance of items which lead to dental dilapidation. The very langwidge acknowledges this - don't it Sugar? And if you ain't Sugar, p'raps you're Honey. OK sweetness? Or is your name Candy?

Why is Hollywood-whiteness abundant? The answer is that in a culture where packaging has as much or more value than content, a few thousand spent at the tooth technician for a bright white smile is a solid investment in your future.

The UK hasn't got there yet. Media personalities here know that a gleaming mouthful is a professional necessity but other prominents haven't caught on. Study the biting gear of politicians next time they are on the box, you'll see what I mean.

Amongst my current entourage, vulnerables, it appears there's a shortage of oral maintenance since mossy molars and off-colour canines are the rule. Nearly all of them smoke and are afeared of the tooth doc. But they must have attended at some point – or else they've come off worse in a brawl – since a wide frontal gap and the consequent mushy diction is common. It gives them an extra weapon should the need arise; I would not like to be bitten by the remaining fangs.

In the long run it makes no odds, the set provided by nature will be extracted and porcelain replacements look luvly. My pal Dave says his dentures 'Are like the stars, they come out at night'.

* * *

Seagulls and Darwin

If you get it to yourself, the kitchen in the Bristol YHA hostel is the best one of all the backpacker hostels around here. There's plenty of space, three fridges, two stoves, two sinks and all the pots and pans you might need. There is one issue however and it pertains throughout the entire YHA network; no adequately sized mugs or glasses.

There may be a good reason, perhaps in the past they had regular size mugs and they disappeared, stolen. Other hostels seem to be able to provide the item - although they have their own peculiar omissions. In the Rock 'n Bowl you're lucky if you can find a full set of cutlery; knives and teaspoons, yes; forks no.

But at 6:45 a.m. I have everything I need for tea and toast. These items prepared, I sit at the counter by the window and break fast.

Another guest arrives, and we exchange 'Good mornings'. This develops to a light chat. His reason for the stay is that he's moving flats and since the out date is a couple of days before the in one, the gap is economically filled by a few nights in the YHA.

I learn that he's an aircraft engineer; lots of those in Bristol, my dad was one, and the British and Colonial Aeroplane Company he worked for is still going; now called British Aircraft Corporation.

This fellow tells me; 'The seagulls find the optimum routings around town, making efficient use of air currents around buildings'. He then went on to tell me something inappropriate for meal times; 'They visit the sewage works, find undigested maize grains and when they've had enough, they head off to a lake to clean themselves up'.

Thank you, I did not wish to know that.

* * *

Emails

I haven't done any paid work for a long time and some cash would come in handy. When this email arrived, it looked for a while as though I might be able to revert to gainful employment.

> Hi Robert,
>
> Hope things are going OK. I don't know if you are able at the moment, but I need some help with Sales and Marketing. I am doing it all myself at the moment and I need someone who can advise on how to get more customers. We can do it with Skype and I will pay for your time.
>
> Cheers,
>
> Michael

But it was not to be. That was a shame, since Mike is an old friend and I owe him bigly.

I know plenty about sales work, so on that level I ought to have been able to help. Trouble is, Mike operates in the Netherlands and his product is a speciality within an area I have no idea about, and frankly am not interested in. But I have another friend who can at least point Mike in the right direction.

> Hi Mark,
>
> My long-time friend Michael, asked me for help with Linkedin as a marketing tool. Unfortunately this is something I know almost nothing about, but you do. Please talk to him as soon as you can.
>
> Robert

The two Ms conversed, after which Mike contacted me again with ideas about how I could collaborate with him. I gave it a try for a week but the fundamentals were staring me in the face; this is a complex topic I know virtually nothing about and I don't speak Dutch. So with a large dollop of regret and much shame I sent him the following.

> Subject: Beekeeping for fish
>
> Hello Mike,
>
> I have been reading up on LinkedIn and playing around with it.
>
> Fish don't know a lot about keeping bees.
> The received opinion of how one should present oneself on this platform conflicts with my present values - I don't want to be 'professional' - 'amusing idiot' is more my goal.
>
> I anticipate that you will tell me that with effort and dedication fish can pick up beekeeping to an adequate level, but I am not sanguine about this.
>
> Do you have any shirts which need ironing? I think I could manage that.
>
> Robert
>
> Sorry sorry .
>
> Really!
>
> ***

* * *

Drink 'n Drugs

A lot of boozing goes on in hostels, both the commercial / backpacker variety and the Council emergency accommodation for vulnerables. Here are some vignettes:

I was in the St. Christopher's, Bath earlier in the year and went up to the small, poorly-furnished, noisy (telly on), in one sense appropriately chilly (windows blocked open), 'chill out' room. There were 4 people sitting 'round the small dining table, three were Americans, one an Ozzie female. The Americans had something about them which made me suspect they were in the military.

One thing which is handy about the St. C. is that food and drink is available directly across the road at Waitrose, a large, expensive, supermarket. The aforementioned bods had been there and spent a lot of money on a collection of spirits, Jack D, of course being one.

There was also a man from Albania with them – 'I'm a chippy he announced' in nearly authentic London dialect.

The business of the night was to consume lotsa alcohol in preparation for going on to a club. This was taken seriously and good progress was made. The Albanian offered encouragement and support to this with tales of his own drinking achievements, the expenditure involved and his tolerance of unusual excess. His tipple for the present evening was a bottle of Famous Grouse. He spoke of customarily paying £45 for vodka.

Spurred on by this, the Oz-girl recounted not just booze epics, she also reviewed an alphabet soup of other mind-altering substances, including most of the following: DET, DMA, DMHP, DMT, DMT, DOB, DOET, DXM, GHB, Ketamine, LSD, MDA, MDE, MDMA, MDMA, Mescaline, Meth, PCE, PCP, Psilocybin.

Unfamiliar acronyms for me apart from LSD. The remainder of the band seemed to follow though.

The British weather on that night was cold and wet; the Albanian announced that in his homeland it was warm and now would be the time of year to harvest lemons. Next day

I had a web-look for myself and it turned out that the chippy chappy was quite wrong it was barely warmer in Tirana than Bristol.

So far I have hinted at the extent of my own drinking - it's not a subject of pride - but my account would be incomplete if I left it out.

I'm a binge drinker not a daily beer-for-breakfast type because the desire for alcohol never comes to me until lunchtime at the earliest. And not every day either because after a heavy night I do not want to know anything more about the Devil's chemical.

But give it 48 hours, the suffering over, and this fool thinks once more, 'What harm can it do?' And then one is both too much and not enough. Just a taste of it and the active ingredient transits from gut to brain in seconds. Then the fuse is lit, more and worse will follow. (Usually, not always).

Bristol is a place where you are never far from a pub, off-license or late-night store. Nor do you need to have much money to indulge. My seven months of research has located two pubs where you can get a pint for two pounds and one cider house where the local apple brew costs just £1.90. Pretty incredible since I know of other locales where you pay twice as much for the same.

In further support of my thesis that '**Y**ou **C**an't **H**ave **E**verything', whilst I longed for something other than Pilsner during my years in Germany, now that I'm back, in the birthplace of Imperial Pale Ale, paying for UK's golden, aromatic nectar is painful.

If you aren't too fussy, in rural Deutschland a null comma fünf litre glass of Bier can be had for one euro fifty – not much more than an one USD or one GBP these Brexit-troubled times.

The worst paying-for-it-moment occurred in the Brew Dog bar on Baldwin Street. They offer a convenient way to sample their beer range, using what they call a 'flight'; it comprises four 1/3 pint measures of different ales on a wooden tray and helps patrons decide which to have more of later. My mood was chipper, I ordered.

Then the sky fell. 'Nine pounds please mate'.

The right thing to do in such circumstance is to say, 'What? I'm not paying that'. Or you could be sly and lie your way out of the problem, 'Left my wallet in the car, back in a moment', and bugger off.

I'm too cowardly and slow for either, I paid-and-regretted.

* * *

Lately I've been hitting the vodka. Why? Initially because what I was trying to do was economise. That is to say in the knowledge that I would be tempted to consume to the point where any more is clearly unwise, I wanted to achieve this with the least expense.

How to accomplish? By smuggling in a quarter, on occasions a half, bottle of spirit to a pub or meeting place and then using that to make a single purchased pint last the entire night. Pretty clever eh?

Unfortunately not that smart, since my glass-boosting manoeuvres were spotted on several occasions by those around me. Not ultimately serious, I escaped being banned from the establishments involved but it made me aware that my efforts at concealment were less effective than I had imagined.

At the Chelsea, where a sizeable throng gathers in the back yard at night and a good deal of Caribbean smoking produce is vaporised I thought that my economy measure would pass without comment.

Wrong.

As Jeff-free (he prefers that spelling) informed, 'If they spot you, you'll get one warning and if there's a next time, that's it, a permanent ban'.

I had what I think is a jolly good idea; the problem for drinkers with a quantity of the strong stuff about their person is getting the fluid from container to mouth, concealed that is.

To facilitate this, I have imagined a flask made and coloured in the likeness of a smart phone. Since everybody from child to grave-dodger has one of these devices they attract no attention. What's more, when speaking you hold them close to your face. All that is needed to achieve device-to-mouth transfer is to have a stubby outlet on which you suck.

My daughter, a product designer, could make me a prototype - although I won't be asking, too much shame - then it could be manufactured in China for tuppence ha'penny and sold in the West for a ten quid or so.

I should give up the drink, but I don't suppose I will, been at it too long, over fifty years now and I have a library of excuses-to-myself. My heroes are / were - since it finished off most of them - dedicated boozers;

- Peter Cook - deemed the wittiest Englishman in history.
- Tommy Cooper, Tony Hancock - both outstandingly funny men.
- Raymond Chandler, acknowledged as one of the greatest exponents of written English.
- P. G. Wodehouse who gave the world Jeeves and Bertie Wooster.
- Richard Burton of single-malt-matured-in-sherry-cask voice.
- Churchill, with his courage, ability in many fields and wonderful oratory.
- Kingsley Amis - author of 'Lucky Jim', 'Difficulties with Girls' and 'On Drink'

I admire them all - and so did the licensed trade.

Intoxication appears firmly linked to creativity and its part in the lives of these great people cannot be denied. I'm not an advocate for boozing, it's unhealthy, expensive and I have a record of stupid acts performed while under the influence. I'll just say that ethyl fumes do seem to attract the Muse and catalyse ideas and often some harmless silliness.

* * *

In the All Hallows hostel there's a ban on alcohol, officially that is. 'We don't care what you do outside. But you can't bring it in here', says Sophie, one of our minders. And then one night, Del has a big bottle and is sharing its contents around, 'Want some lemonade, Rob?'

'Yes please'.

He pours me a cupful and I taste it. 'This is cider, not lemonade.' I say not in a whisper.

And Sophie, who is sitting in the office with the door open, roars, 'You drinking cider?'

I respond with a feeble, 'No Sophie, my mistake, it's lemonade'.

Del says, 'I thought you was street-wise enough to know better Rob'.
I had the wrong type of education; to learn basic urban life-skills, always choose an Approved School.

A bit late in this narrative - I should have told you earlier - that the English South West is cider country and it's a very popular drink here. There are plenty of varieties; the one with the longest pedigree is called 'Scrumpy', also known as rough cider.

You can immediately tell that it's not anodyne for-the-masses cordial, there's a clear hint of a compound which warns that however much you like the taste and immediate effect, less would be wiser than more. I wouldn't chance anything beyond two pints. Foolish souls who do, will not be enjoying their next morrow.

* * *

Drugs 'n Drink

Apart from ethyl alcohol I'm not into drugs, and from what I see of the people around me that is very lucky.

'Spiced-up' individuals, might as well be dead, that's how they look to me zonked out on pavements and benches. Particularly affecting is the sight of one nineteen year-old who reminds me in his build and hairstyle of my younger son, as he was a dozen years ago.

This young man often isn't able to communicate normally, being so doped up. When he can talk he seems intelligent and interested in the things which usually appeal to people of his age. The last time I saw him, he was slumped in an armchair, barely conscious.

I would like to help; getting him out of his present surroundings to a completely different existence might be a way which could bring change. A job on a farm, working with animals or plants, might give him enough satisfaction to be able to quit drugs.

I have no expertise in this area - he is seeing professionals who do, or who ought to have, but whatever approach they are using, it's not working; a big shame.

In this house, we have alcoholics, opiate-users, spice and weed-smokers. K. is on the vodka as soon as he wakes up in the morning. J. says 'It steadies him'. B. likes his dooby, he tells us, and the smell fills the backyard and drifts into the house.

I'm getting tired of that pungent herb odour, it's everywhere in Bristol. Recently Peter Hitchens had a tirade in his Daily Mail column about exactly this. Normally I disagree with him, but on this point we are as one.

Some nights I'm lying in bed and the smell comes into my room under the door. Man I wish I had my own place and not here, somewhere else. I miss the fresh air of my previous home in Germany.

But you can't have everything.

***

The business of homelessness

It's too late for me to start another biz venture and besides, I don't really want to since I have other things to do with my remaining years. But from what I have seen of providing accommodation for vulnerables, it looks like a winner.

A successful business offers a product that its market wants and is prepared to pay for. So who wants housing for people who have no home of their own and who aren't good at fending for themselves? Answer: public bodies which are legally required to provide it; and as far as this concerns me, it's Bristol City Council.

How strong is the demand? Plenty strong. Between the people who move here because of the city's attractions and opportunities for work; immigrants from abroad; and those offloaded here by other housing authorities, there are many people needing somewhere to live. This means that property owners can charge high rents and be choosy about who they let in. Age, sub 40, over 20, employed with good references, is the standard landlords are looking for.

This leaves out a rather large chunk of humanity; say you are 19 no job, no bank account, no savings and no one helping you, how are you going to get somewhere? At the other end of the age scale it's no different, forget finding a private place.

These imperfects, are not wanted and some of them manage somehow to exist with a life of begging, charitable kitchens and shop doorways. Tents are another choice and you see them in odd spots around the town; one guy camps on a narrow overgrown ledge by the side of the river Avon, adjacent to Spike Island, the latter a place constructed to appeal to tourists and where a sandwich costs a fiver. For a couple of weeks there were two tents on College Green, a location so prominent that it pressured the authorities to expedite a better alternative for the peeps in question.

One weekend in the winter I went over to Cardiff because I couldn't find anywhere affordable in Bristol/Bath and surrounds. On street corners and in front of empty shops there were tents all over. Someone told me the local council was giving them out as a home substitute. What next, a cardboard box?

Then there are all the vans and caravans to be seen in any less-than-posh parts; alongside the motorway there are many, in leafier districts too. Unsurprisingly adjacent property owners don't like this; it would be difficult to argue that it's a pleasing sight when a van-dweller pours a bucket of shit and piss down the drain outside your dwelling. But what else are the poor bastards supposed to do?

There is not enough social housing and nothing much is being done about it. A major cause was the 'Right to buy' policy in the Thatcher years when council tenants by buying their homes were decreasing the stock of social housing. This motivated as much for party political advantage as small c conservative values.

Behind the apparent generosity of permitting tenants to become owners on advantageous terms lay the darker reason for the policy, it was expected that it would lead to an increase in the number of voters for the Conservative party.

More recently 'Buy to let', although purported to be a way to increase the number of accommodations available to those who are not able to buy, has brought about a sharp rise in rents. The rent controls of fifty years ago have been long abandoned.

With the shortage of rental properties, private tenants today are in a weak position if they want to have deficiencies in their homes fixed. Landlords can force them to quit by saying that they need the property empty in order to carry out renovations.

What to do about this problem? You might make a well-considered plan and implement it promptly and effectively - or you could throw money at it. Option one is difficult, so choice two is what the Council and national government go with.

Which takes us back to the business of homelessness; there's a nice amount of money to be made if you help the poor old Council meet its obligations. Where I stay, the house is one of several owned by a company which offers the Council accommodation for people who fit the 'vulnerable' category.

It's nominally B&B, only we don't get B #2, nevertheless it's not cheap. Or rather it's exceptionally cheap for us the occupants, all we pay is £15.60 a week, and that's for heat, light, water. The single occupancy room, kitchen, laundry, cleaning and staff services are all free - to us that is.

The Council though, is paying £40 a night per person.

Make a spreadsheet, take it to a bank and ask for a loan, the bank will like the look of these figures. Here's the maths.

I'm describing one house here; it's big and has two extensions each of which have a common room and a kitchen, so it was an expensive property to buy and convert, but now look at the cash flow it generates which is staggering.

Eighteen rooms at 40 pounds a night, if they are all occupied - they are currently - makes £720. So in a month of 30 days, that works out to £21,600.

Over a year let's round the total to £260,000.

Subtract the running costs; a couple of staff in shifts for most of the day, utilities, insurance, maintenance, rates, replacement of furnishings, a van. If this doesn't leave you with 100 grand, you shouldn't be in business.

Assuming it does, the bank will be delighted to let you have the necessary to buy a handful more properties, after all the source of this lovely income isn't ordinary, potentially unreliable renters, no it's the local agent for Her Majesty's Government.

What's not to like? Everybody gets what they want, it's win/win. Or rather win cubed since it's good for three parties; the property co; the Council, since it's their problem sorted; and the homeless oiks, who get an upgrade from tent or shop doorway. So everybody's happy.

Or so it would be easy to think. But hold on, where is the source of this river of dosh? Do I hear someone say, 'The Government'?

But where does H.M.G. get it? Oh, er, ah, em, would that be from the taxpayers? It would. And are these funders getting value for money? No, not really.

What brings this home is a term I came across in a newspaper article - 'benefits farming'. It implies that the system I have roughly described can be seen in the same sort of light as farmers who receive an EEC grant to NOT plant certain crops. It's a fiddle, easy money for the providers and in the same value category for the taxpayers as MPs expenses. Need I mention moat-cleaning, duck houses or staff salaries paid to a relative?

But what to do about it? And what should be the scope of the debate? Should we widen the question and ask, 'Is poverty forever, or do we want to eliminate it?'

A suggestion I came across which would help is that no one should own more than one property until everybody has a home. I've put this idea to a number of people and most have endorsed it. One man didn't; referring to multi-residence owners, 'If they've worked hard and got the money, why shouldn't they have other properties?'

To me this reasoning attempts to justify inequality. And if some inequality is OK, is there any reason to limit it? Could society be comprised of just two classes, billionaires and beggars? Was Thatcher right in 1987 saying 'There is no such thing as society'?

If you take a 'utilitarian' line of reasoning, you can make the case that a tiny number of very rich people and a large majority of poor ones makes for a great waste of resources.

We exist in a knowledge economy; the industrial revolution, manufacturing and manual labour belong to previous eras. To participate in the 'knowledge economy', the fundamental is to possess knowledge, which is what the education system exists for.

Since poor people currently receive less education than the wealthy, they are less able to work in roles where they can contribute significantly.

Leave people ignorant, through lack of education and not only are they unable to do valuable work, more money is required to assist them with housing, health and other problems.

I feel I'm too old to enter politics, but if I did, my platform would be to strive for a society which provides decent housing, health and education for all.

* * *

Dealing with the Council

If you seek help from the Council, it can become tempting to feel that it's 'them versus me'. In fairness one has to accept that they have other categories of problem to address in addition to housing. What's more, attempting to fix a huge problem caused by national government policy will inevitably lead to difficult compromises and stopgap 'fudges'.

The first thing to try and grasp is that when you enter the social welfare system, you give up your autonomy. From now on it won't be you making decisions; it will be 'The Council', a monolith on which you can bring very little influence to bear. You will be told how it's going to be; what you want won't have much weight.

The 'sword of Damocles' dangling by a thread over your neck is that if the Council deems that 'you have made yourself voluntarily homeless' then they can just tell you 'we cannot help you' - and then you must sort yourself out as best you can.

This same sanction applies to offers of accommodation - you'd better accept what you are offered or else. 'Else' meaning you are kicked out of the system. There is an appeals process, but myself I hope to never get to that point.

Of course there is one avenue still open as suggested earlier by Del - get yourself arrested and imprisoned for a short spell on a minor offence and when you come out, you're top of the list and will be offered a place to stay. Bingo! A good proportion of fellow residents in All Hallows arrived by this route.

This brings with it the more or less automatic consequence that if you want anything better than 'take it or leave it' options from the Council, you need to learn the ways in which you can 'game' the system. That is, use tactics which conform to the Council's requirements but which in some manner get you closer to what you would like.

There's a useful primer detailing what is significant in this area; the manual intended for Council staff guidance, surprisingly it is available online to anyone who cares to look it up.

This document describes the obligatory duties of the Council towards people who are seeking help. With this are also the requirements that such applicants must fulfil. It also specifies those things which are not taken into consideration - to me a surprise was that age alone is not viewed as a significant factor.

Those which are important are all associated with **VULNERABILITY**.

This in capitals since it is at the core of what you need to be clued up on.

What contributes to **big V**?

- Under 18
- Woman with child(ren)
- Fleeing violence
- Recently released from
  - prison with likelihood of re-offending
  - mental hospital
  - hospital (with serious condition and no home)
  - drug/alcohol rehab clinic
- Serious health problems making life on the street dangerous
- Mental health problems – depression, risk of suicide
- A provable history of living on the street

These are the principal factors, and if you want to enter the social welfare system, you will be at a disadvantage if you do not present some of them when you apply.
If this is new to you, as it was for me, a good source of information is to talk to street people. I have found that they are generally quite happy to share with you what they know.

There's a caveat though, each individual you ask will have a background containing factors specific to him or her, so you should not assume that advice given will necessarily work for you. But by asking a good number of people, you'll be able to piece together what is likely to be applicable in your own case.

If there is no urgent factor making you go to the Council immediately, do this research early, it should stop you from saying something which will disadvantage you.

At Council interviews if you are asked a question which you suspect may have a critical bearing on your chances, you can always reply, 'I don't really know, I'm a bit confused'. There are enough people that Council staff see who have impaired memories due to drug and alcohol use that this answer is common and cannot be refuted.

* * *

Timing and residency

I'm not going to encourage you to dishonesty, but there are some issues where rules can be bent if not broken. For example, the requirement to be resident for a minimum of six months in order to be considered for Emergency Housing.

During that period, you aren't confined to barracks or under house arrest, you may perfectly well have a principal abode in the local area but from time to time be away to visit family and friends.

Contrast this with the regime which applies when you have entered the Emergency Housing accommodation; in this you are in effect under curfew, since you will be signing a form saying that you will always return to your accommodation by midnight. And although hostel staff appear to let some residents get away with being absent for a night or two, there would probably be trouble if an incident occurred and higher management got to know about it.

Another tip is to obtain a written record of any medical condition. Doctors will provide a summary which can be shown to Council staff. It's a general point that any aspect of your life which tends to increase your chances of acceptance will have greater influence if documented rather than offered verbally.

This relates to an important point; viewed from the perspective of the Council employee, what they have to do in 'processing' you is to make sure that any decision or action that they take can be justified – it must conform to the guidelines under which they operate.

This brings us to another big and important term,

ACCOUNTABILITY.

Council staff tend to be 'jobsworth' types, meaning that they know - and perhaps fear - that their employment is conditional on not breaking the rules.

This factor accounts for procedures which appear to go against logic. For example, there was a time in my backpacker hostel period where the amount of Housing Benefit which I was receiving was substantially less than I was actually paying each night and week. I went to the Council to report this and ask for my payment to be adjusted up towards the real cost.

What actually happened was a surprise, a nasty one. The Council lady heard what I had to say and responded by telling me that her first action would be to cancel my Housing Benefit payments. They would resume later, four weeks or so on, but for the interim, if I wanted to stay in hostels, I would need to pay for them myself.

Obviously this was a bit of a shock to me, since I was only just covering my non-rent living expenses; a week's money would be gone by the end of the seven days. No way to finance myself for a month. I put this to the Council lady, she was unmoved, and that was that.

Luckily I had been helped with a previous difficulty by another Council employee and seeing him at the other side of the room, I discreetly moved across and when he was free I asked him if he could assist me again.

He told me, 'What my Council colleague has done is correct according to the rules, but I can see that it places you in an impossible situation. Because of that I can take action under a different category, so don't worry, you'll continue to get the money you have been receiving so far'.

Then a few weeks later it did increase in line with what I was actually paying to the hostels.

* * *

A Terrible Tuesday

A question in All Hallows which never gets a satisfactory answer is 'Where am I going next and when?' We all ask it and we all have to settle for the same, 'Nobody knows'.

You can ask the AH staff, you can ask at the Council, you can refer to the experiences of fellow vulnerables, but there is never clarity or certainty.

What officials tell you is couched in generalities and conditional language - 'should be', 'ought to be', 'hopefully'. These responses derive from the hierarchical management structure, where decisions always come from above and the functionaries in the level you have access to plain do not know. They wait for a directive to be handed down from their superiors.

Although this management style conflicts with current thinking about what makes stakeholders happy, maybe experience has shown that it results in the least problems.

For the level of staff that you will be interfacing with it definitely has one advantage; those delivering the 'Dunno' answers can't be held personally responsible. 'Not up to me mate. Sorry.'

With time, you get to the point where 'Inshallah', or your preferred equivalent, has to satisfy.

I'd already served 10 weeks when a remarkable thing happened, my phone rang and a man introduced himself, 'I'm Aaron from Self-Help Housing Association, we are going to offer you accommodation'.

I wasn't expecting this and was momentarily discombobulated, but I still managed to ask a few questions; 'What, where, when?' and received brief, disappointingly uninformative answers and an invitation to attend their office for an 'assessment'. This term being another with Council-specific meaning; it's an important word in a vulnerable's lexicon.

At this point in my odyssey it would be assessment number four. Pretty well the same questions are asked each time, and it takes good recall to be able to provide consistent answers. I don't know whether this is done for the same purpose that the cops do it, or it could be just redundant repetition. When friendly policeman and nasty policeman perform their double act, the idea is to see whether your story is genuine - and to break your defences if it isn't.

I did my best to offer the exact same info that I had on the other occasions, but wasn't sure just how much emphasis to put on the jolly old mental (in)stability and urge-to-drink topics. I had the impression that mental stuff could perhaps give me a kind-of legitimate out if the place offered wasn't to my liking. I was wrong.

I hadn't paid sufficient attention when being coached on this by fellow All Hallows residents. They told me 'It's no good saying, I don't like the street /room/other occupants' – your personal taste in such things doesn't count. It's physical defects you really need.

If you can't climb the stairs or step into the bath tub, these health handicaps must be considered.

I'd primed Dr. Will on my tendency to mental highs and lows, but now I needed something in writing to list the body defects. Fortunately it turned out that it's something your doc will give you just for the asking.

In answer to Aaron's question 'How do you behave when you are feeling depressed?' I replied. 'I tend to go to bed and stay there for a long time; until the mood has passed. That can be a couple of days sometimes.' I thought I was safe with that. Aaron did not comment.

The session concluded with a remark which surprised me, 'We'll consider what you've told us and see if we can make you an offer. Should be able to let you know on Friday'.

'What, you told me you were offering me accommodation. Is this now uncertain?' - I thought to myself.

The lack of definite offer was particularly significant, since when I returned to All Hallows a letter from the Council was waiting for me. Amongst a lot of boiler plate, justifying the Council's actions and decisions, was a sentence telling me that consequent on the housing association offer , the Council's 'Duty of Care' towards me was about to be discharged.

Translated this means, 'You're on your own now, we've done all we are required to'. The Council Homeless dept were hereby washing its hands of Robert.

A couple of days came and went without further contact from Council or Housing Assoc. Fine, I am happy enough in All Hallows – conditions could be, have been, far worse.

On Friday, I stayed close to my phone anticipating a call. Nope, nothing. So at quarter to five in the afternoon, I called them. 'Hello Aaron, I just wanted to make sure that I hadn't missed a call from you today.' I hadn't.

'Sorry about that, should be able to let you know by midday Monday', he said.

It wasn't a relaxing weekend; I wanted to know their decision since it concerned the setting for the next months and perhaps years of my life. The following Monday it was another anxious wait for a phone call – which also didn't come. This time around I didn't call them; instead I waited until the following day and wrote a note to my Council Housing Officer.

To my surprise I received a prompt and helpful answer, saying 'Sorry you have been messed around, I'll look into this. You can stay in All Hallows until we have an alternative for you.'

So no urgent need to worry about where I will pass the night – fine, I'm writing a book and the institutional life is very suitable for that. Living somewhere a bit free-er of the crazies would be nice, but I can hold out OK.

A week goes by and then I'm told to attend the housing association's office on the coming Tuesday for a visit to a property they will be offering me. This is exciting; in the interval, I make a recce out to the St Pauls area, which is where this offered place is located. I've asked what AH residents think of that district, and no one has much good to say, it's got a bit of a rep.

But on Monday evening what I see there looks perfectly OK, if anything a degree cleaner and ordered than Easton my current locus. Getting to the new part of town is a bit tricky, there's a major highway cutting through the area, separating my present address from the tentative future one.

Googling and zooming in at high magnification reveals a footpath going through a park and crossing the River Frome. This does make direct access possible; otherwise, it would have to be a bus into The Centre then another one back out again on the far side of the motorway, a bit of a faff.

So by bus and some map-reading, I reach the path and its surrounding park. I stop for a while to look at the Frome River; it's in a culvert – if that's the word. There are high walls on either side of a small but lively stream; a good place for nature to do its thing. Lots of water plants, I'd imagine fish too, although I don't see any. Two ducks have nice accommodation atop a shopping trolley. The birds, heads under their wings, are snoozing peacefully.

A hundred metres further, there's a footbridge across the motorway, approaching it, the traffic roar increases unpleasantly and the air stinks. Not good if my next res. is close to this – and it probably wouldn't be an allowable refusal factor either.

On the far side of the bridge I ask a man if he's local, he is, and ask which way to walk to reach the heart of St. Pauls. He indicates a direction; I proceed and am liking what I see. In contrast to Easton, where the streetscape is principally small houses, flash motors outside and geezers without jobs driving them badly, this is almost yuppie territory. No SUVs or bins on the pavements, the front yards are cared-for and so far not a single grotfito.

There's a community centre incorporating a library; in the opposite direction a row of small independent shops. I'm about to cross a road, when two cyclists stop in front of me and discuss something in French. I seize the opportunity to ask in that lingo if there's a decent pub in the area. They do not know, they are visitors.

Now a man in a white robe calls to me also in French. I ask him if he's of that nationality; he isn't, he's from Palestine. Ali's been living in St Pauls for nine years. We continue in English – I tell him that I will be moving to the area shortly and ask him how he likes living here. He tells me that it is much better these days. The anti-socials have been displaced by families who are well-behaved. That's good to hear. We walk together for several streets, until at City Road, he says, 'This is where I live'; we shake hands and say goodbye.

Now for the first time I recognise where I am and it's off to one side of Stokes Croft – hipster central. There are plenty of attractive shops, pubs, restaurants, cafes and other facilities within that area but smart it isn't. Midnight aerosol artists, fly-posters, restaurants putting out their empties and overflowing garbage bins see to that. Yuck.

In Paris, they wash the streets early every morning. I invite the relevant Bristol authority to take a trip there and see if that isn't nicer.
I know that by making such comment I reveal to the 'alternative' world that my values are 'misaligned', I am judging on superficialities; art, creative freedom, self-expression are where it's really at.

If I could safely transit Stokes Croft with eyes shut, that's what I'd do, but it has a busy road going right through it, causing polluted air and pedestrian danger.

Now I'm in need of a drink and a sit-down so I take a brief look in the Grand Temple of Cool – Hamilton House which also goes by the handle 'The Canteen'. Although the hundred or so clients are intent on their device screens they are keeping some chat going too, the place is noisy. It's also hot and the lighting gloomy. Add to that the food and drink is expensive and I'm asking myself, Why did I bother?' To go in, that is, since it's always like this.

Some phenomena defy rational explanation. The Canteen is pretty horrible by 'normal' standards yet is a place of devoted popularity amongst the locals. Is this inverted snobbery, as per that offensive fashion, 'ripped' jeans?

De toute façon I'm in and out of there PDQ then cross the road to The Crofters Rights, a spacious bar with a wide selection of real ales. Half an hour couch time, one nice local IPA, and I feel restored.

* * *

Next day, fateful Tuesday, I make myself as presentable as I can, given that I've been living out of a small suitcase for months now, then I head in to town once more. Fifteen minutes early, I hang around on a corner until most of that interval has elapsed, and then I walk up King Square Avenue and buzz the intercom.

Aaron greets me, guides me into a waiting room and showing me a form asks, 'See if there is anything you want on this list'. They're basic household articles, cooking and sleeping gear mostly. The prices of the items are listed and are remarkably low. 'We can give you up to twenty pounds' worth'.

Since I have none of the items on this paper, I tell him I could use everything. So then he says 'I'll go and see what we've got'.

A few minutes later he returns with a brand new duvet, pillow, covers and frying pan. 'That's all I could find'. A little pointless to ask me my choice then. I let that pass, mustn't be churlish.

Then we bundle the freebies into his car and head for the place I will shortly be calling home – presumably.

The route retraces much of the path I walked the previous night and when we turn off City Road, I recognise that this is close to the Anarchists' cafe, a place I visited in the winter for a cheap meal and a heated conversation.

I'll go back if I'm living nearby, although ultimately it's futile talking about a better world; the unscrupulous bastards at the top always construct a society where it's the rich what gets the pleasure and it's the poor what gets the blame. Ain't it all a bloody shame?

We're heading towards the motorway I crossed last night, not good. But we turn off a couple of hundred metres before it and stop at the end of this street. The address we are going to is right in front. From outside it looks alright, it's outside I like, it's an acceptable outside, I say to myself 'This outside is alright', trouble is . . .

(Millenials I apologise for the above. I couldn't help it; my words are a cheap copy of lines in a sketch by Peter Cook, my great hero. They just flew out of my head onto screen. Couldn't stop them. Sorry.)

And the trouble began once the front door was open and we entered. A bare wood floor featuring flyers for pizza, taxis and betting and mail addressed to 'occupier'; a narrow hall; stairs, a passage to the kitchen at the rear and everything left, right, up, down dirty, grimy, neglected, abused.

We go up the stairs and enter the bathroom first. The WC pan has that dark brown ring of shit-stained scale which tells you when cleaning was last performed - never. There's a bath with a shower hose laying in it, the curtain is hanging off at an angle and a window no cleaner has touched this decade.

Now the bedroom; there's a bare mattress on a double bed, a chest of drawers, two chairs and another dirty window, illumination by naked central light bulb.

Have you seen Scorsese's early triumph – Taxi Driver, where De Niro as Travis, the lead character, lives in a New York flop house? This Cairns Crescent, Bristol BS2 location would have served equally well.

I begin my protest; 'This is horrible'. It evokes a defensive response, 'They're all like this. It's what you get. It may not be luxury, we don't promise you that'.

I am not surprised by Aaron's remark but I am really taken aback by the very poor condition of this place. I was not expecting it. I have seen conditions like this before; London had slum areas when I was growing up, I've been in squats – visiting, I have never lived in one. I don't want to now.

We go back down the stairs and to the kitchen at the rear. It's down one step from the hall and cramped. You couldn't fit three people into it, two would be tight. The counters are loaded with dirty pans and plates in piles; the sink is full of the same, floating in greasy water. There's a small fridge and next to it a bucket with rubbish overflowing on to the floor. The stove top is black with carbonised food.

I'm supposed to share this with three other people.

There's a door to a back yard. Outside there is an area which could be made pleasant with a lot of work and some investment, but there hasn't been either. Instead broken paving, thistles to waist height and a pan of food + rainwater, which is fermenting nicely.

There's a side wall to the street since this house is on a corner. That's not good, you wouldn't need to be an athlete to scale it, I could at a push. Having previously lived in two corner houses, I know that they are particularly vulnerable to burglars. The back door would give with one serious kick, the bedroom door too and my computer would be away to fund an addict's next fix.

I'm in a bit of a daze at all this decrepitude and the idea that it is 'suitable' housing. Fortunately I still have the instinct to take some photos. I do that but it's not easy to capture the filthy feel of the place. If there is a next time, video might be better; you can pan around to show the scene more completely. We finish the tour and outside Aaron asks me what I think.

'It's horrible but I don't have any choice do I? If I refuse it, you'll make me homeless. I know that.'

Aaron says that he agrees with me about the condition. I ask him if he considers the place 'suitable' and he says that it isn't, but that's the offer – take it or . . .

I say that I will take it; I can't face returning to the backpacker hostel conditions. In the car, returning to the office to sign the paperwork I go over this continuously. Am I really going to live in that shithole? Before we reach destination I know that I won't.

We arrive and get out of the car, Aaron opens up the office and ushers me in. I take a couple of steps in that direction and then it floods out of me, 'No, I'm not living in that squalor. I don't give a damn if that makes me homeless'.

Aaron repeats the bromide, 'That's your decision'. I'm sick of hearing that phrase, 'Yes that's right; it's what I've decided'. I would have liked to add 'You cunt', somehow I find the restraint not to.

He tries one more 'If that's your decision' and although I would have loved to sock him one in the kisser I turn and walk. Shaken.

The journey back to All Hallows my emotions were in wild turmoil, my heart racing. I knew what was ahead of me in the next hours - packing, goodbyes and re-entry to backpacker life.

Staying in hostels when you are holidaying is one thing; when it's your indefinite future, a quite different other. I'd escaped from it three months ago – a blessed relief, and now I was returning. Jesus fucking H. Fuck, fuck, fuck.

Even just writing about it one week later, much of that feeling comes back to me. Man, my fucking life!

* * *

Well that part was fun . . . and it didn't stop there.

I wandered in a daze and light rain to the bus stop then travelled back towards All Hallows. It was pouring down by the time I got off, so I hurried across the road and sheltered in the doorway of a building opposite. When the worst of the weather had passed, I moved on towards my shortly-to-be former address.

My shirt was soaked by the time I got there and I felt hungry, exhausted and unable to think straight. Despite that I felt very aggrieved that I have to choose between squalor and homelessness, and I forced myself to write a note to the Council Homeless team.

> Dear Ms. K,
>
> I viewed 29 Cairns Crescent, St Agnes this morning.
>
> The overall condition of the parts of the house that I saw is poor. Throughout the house there is an air of neglect.
>
> The bathroom is not clean, the toilet stained and evidently not cleaned thoroughly for a long time. The kitchen is also unclean, and unhygienic; dirty dishes and pans on the counter and in sink; a bucket overflowing with rubbish on the floor.
>
> I suffer periodically from depression; I know that I would have thoughts of suicide if I was compelled to live in such conditions.
>
> If you decide that I am hereby making myself voluntarily homeless, so be it. I refuse to live in such a dirty place.
>
> Best regards,
>
> Robert Leslie

Time is pressing, I know that the AH staff will soon be chasing me to quit room and hostel – because, heartless as it seems, that's management policy.

It comes down, ultimately to money. Once an accommodation offer has been refused, the 'Duty of Care' finishes and the Council will not be paying the accommodation provider. So it's 'Out'. 'Now'.

Eighty years ago, in another place, the Gestapo used to shout another word for this, *'Raus'*.

One week later, I learn that Dee defied a management order; she has left me undisturbed because she could see just how desperate a state I was in. Her immediate colleague Sophie, less directed by human kindness, was urging Dee to get me gone, pronto.

On the day, after forty five minutes of rest, I can begin the packing; it's actually more a matter of triage, lots of my belongings will have to be abandoned. If I'm going to the Rock 'n Bowl hostel, there is no storage space in the dorms, one case and a backpack is it, anything else will be too much to carry and a nuisance.

An hour into this, my phone sounds and there's a text from the Housing Officer at Bristol Council –

> We looked into this matter and have concluded that the accommodation was unsuitable. We will make you one more offer, until then you can remain in All Hallows.

This reversal, wonderful though it was, meant I had to now press a mental undo button and cancel the frantic actions of the previous moments. It was too much, overwhelming; anguish, disbelief, deliverance - as of a prisoner awaiting execution, reprieved in the last instant.

When my elation and relief had subsided somewhat, I realised that a battle had been won, but the war wasn't over since if Aaron's remark 'They are all like this', referring to 29 Cairns Cresc. was accurate, the next offer might be no better than what I had just declined.

The more I thought about that the more urgent it was to strengthen my case for being housed somewhere decent. So I worked up the following letter.

Dear Ms. K,

Thank you for your letter and text of 21 June.

As you will know, the majority of today's advertisements for rooms or flatshare specify age limits, typically up to 35, occasionally ten years more. Similarly, Housing Benefit claimants are generally not accepted. This gives licence to unscrupulous landlords to offer squalid housing, given the 'one refusal and you are homeless' policy.

Also, in your words, 'No one expects or wants to cause an affront to your dignity', thank you for the consideration, although I care less about my dignity than my security and health – the principal concerns I had with the offer made last week.

Thank you again,

Robert Leslie

. . . and two things happened;

    1. I didn't get a reply,

2. I got a really great place to live.

After that I had to go out, get away from the hostel, see other things; stop thinking. I walked up the road, into The Queens Head and ordered a pint and made to pay for it.

No wallet!

Not in the usual pocket, nor any other. 'Must have left it at the hostel', I think, telling the barman that I will return.

Back in my room, I look in the spot where I usually hide it if I'm going to be absent for a time. It's not there, or in any other clothing, or on the floor or in my suitcase or my rucksack. I empty everything on to the bed and check carefully item by item. The wallet is definitely not there.

Maybe I dropped it in the street. So I retrace my path, scrutinising the road and pavement. No sign of it and in any case, the school day is over and gaggles of uniformed children are mobile, with young sharp eyes, they'd likely see it and then who knows what they'd do.

Resigned to the loss, the next urgency is to call my bank and get my card cancelled. That goes easily and there is a promise of a replacement in a few days. Well the situation isn't good but thank God it's not on top of being homeless. I've been spared that.

* * *

An uncertain time

Reprieved, at least until the next time. And when might that be, 24 hours or 24 days? – after all I had been in All

Hallows for 11 weeks before the first housing offer came along.

There's no telling about such things, if there is anyone within Council or the housing association surrogates who knows, they keep it closely guarded. What reason there could be for secrecy, I can't guess.

If they did let TempEmergAccom residents have a hint, even if not a precise date, it would give those unfortunates some feeling that things were going to get better before long. As far as I know, that would cost nothing, why not do it?

Some preparations had already been made; my belongings had been subjected to a triage the other day, so I could quickly make ready for another departure.

And I only had myself to think about.

Dee tells me that she has seen the 'instant homelessness' verdict delivered on families with small children. What kind of bastard makes such a policy and thinks it's a good idea?

Wait, that question has an easy answer – look over to the other side of the Atlantic and you'll see.

Another factor would be of greater significance if faced again with 'accept or be evicted'; at least I had been through that once and done the consequent frantic thinking. Now I had a plan of sorts – first head to the Rock 'n Bowl and check in there. Next to the Council to apply for

Housing Benefit, and then look for accommodation of another category.

Once you start to think in a more general way about the value of practising for disasters, it's easy to see the benefits. I might never have arrived at this perspective in normal circumstance, now though I could see that a rehearsal is a good idea. And to have plans B and C.

And here's one of those: I haven't mentioned this so far, but in one of my hostel stays I met an American who was travelling the world as a house-sitter. I have long been interested in doing this myself. There are many appealing aspects; for example, it's likely that you'll be staying in pleasant, occasionally luxurious, homes. There is a demand for house-sitters in many countries a person might want to visit, but where paying rent for your own temporary place to stay would be prohibitive, New York, for one.

The American gave me a few hints; you need a good profile - story and photo, together with appropriately positive testimonials from the property owners you have previously served. The first gig is the hardest to land, after that it's not too difficult. He also said that women get jobs easier than men.

Understandably there are some restrictions on your lifestyle; you can't throw parties, and you can't be absent from the property for very long. These are well compensated by living in nice surroundings and having the possibility to get on with some other activity - perfect for a writer.

Now I recall meeting another person who lives this house-hopping life almost continuously. I encountered her in the Cheddar (of cheese fame) YHA a couple of years ago. She too had told me about the benefits above and in addition said that often house-owners will say, 'Help yourself to any food and drink we've left'. She gets paid too sometimes.

On the website portal where those offering and those seeking engagements can find each other, you can select 'Paid jobs' - presumably there are fewer of these and the clients rather choosy, but the lady I met gets some.

Because I had already sent a detailed letter which expressed my position to the Council Housing Dept. I resisted phoning to ask for further information. Written docs have more impact than speech because they are an enduring record, remarks made in speech can be 'walked back' too easily so are less reliable.

While all this was going on I was still attending the Boots G.P. Surgery (a term for a regular medical facility in the UK). I told Dr. Will what had happened and that I was waiting for a response to my letter. 'You'll be lucky' he said. (Americans, this is irony, a speech device common in the UK.)

The doctor went on to say that in an earlier stage of his career he had worked in the Council section which deals with medical care of homeless people. He knew whereof he spoke.

He was right, no reply came. I developed theories why. It might have been that the points I had raised were not really answerable – that is to say, an attempt in writing to justify bad policy would only make the badness or defects more conspicuous.

Alternatively, the workload that faces Council functionaries might be such that my issue was now low down in the pile.

Ten days went by without reply to my letter and I settled back into a routine. Mornings were occupied with further writing of this account, and then around noon I'd begin preparation for lunch; with that consumed, a siesta, and finally late p.m. shopping, chatting with the other Vulnerables and most likely a trip to one of the local pubs. And repeat - the institutional existence; which for a writer or layabout is easy to take.

There is one disturbing factor that you'll be obliged to live with though; noisy, chaotic nighttimes. It's a comforting precaution to make absolutely certain that your door is secure while you sleep since just outside the aggressives roam.

One thin man, legs ugly with tatts and scabs, likes to wander the upper floors pounding on the doors of those he dislikes. Raha too, changes into her persona as the day ends. She is one who never finds a need to whisper; days she is loud, nights she roars.

Usually it is other women receiving her displeasure, but recently the thin man just mentioned has been target. Since the landing outside of my room often serves as setting for these performances. I carefully turn the lock on my door as far as it will go and plan, if necessary, to use my bed as additional barricade.

That ought to hold until the cops arrive. They're familiar with the address; it never takes them too long.

After one action-packed weekend, during which Blackbeard-the-Flasher has top billing, a couple who room on the top floor, describe a curious phenomenon. 'We're opposite Raha and we can hear three people in her room; three different voices. But when she comes out and her door is open, there's only been one person in the room.'

Maria lives on the same side, the room next to Raha; she says she's heard the voices too. I haven't come across this before. I'm going to look up what Google has to say about 'multiple personality. Using that search term on the NHS website, under the heading 'Dissociative disorders', I find this:

> *Dissociation is a way the mind copes with too much stress. People who dissociate may feel disconnected from themselves and the world around them. Periods of dissociation can last for a relatively short time (hours or days) or for much longer (weeks or months). It can sometimes last for years, but usually if a person has other dissociative disorders. Many people with a dissociative disorder have had a traumatic event during childhood. They may dissociate and avoid dealing with it as a way of coping with it.*

Raha has been through a lot, although you wouldn't guess that to look at her daytime. She is tall, elegant and has a gift for dressing well. I can't see how she can have much money; nevertheless she always wears attractive outfits.

In the last weeks she has been friendly towards me. I had until then kept my distance and said polite 'Good mornings' and 'hellos' nothing more than that because I had seen her displays of temper and was trying not to be caught up in one.

But to my surprise, late one morning, while pounding this keyboard, she came around to the not-used-much-by-residents common room where I sit and work and offered me a small plate of cooked food and a slice of bread. It was good. I reciprocated a few days later with a dish I cooked. From that point on she became quite chatty with me.

If traumatic events lead to bizarre behaviour, Raha had mitigation for her night time craziness. Her story contained these elements; a husband who treated her badly, took her children away telling them that their mother was dead; she/they moved to Sweden as refugees, for some reason that was unsatisfactory, so she came to the UK. Her children are with her mother now. I didn't grasp where that is; I don't think Raha gets to see them.

Dee says about Raha, 'She's on something - class As'.

I don't know if that's true, but the chances are - Dee has had years of experience with disturbed people of all types.

So, if you'll accept that life+crazies can be called normal, mine was rolling along day by unexceptional day. Then the phone rang.

* * *

'Robert we're going to make you another offer', said housing association Aaron. This time we'll come to you, the house is in the same road that you are living in.

I offered thanks and we agreed a time and meeting place, 'On the corner by the school'.

I asked if the house was one of those opposite the school, since I know Clarky one of the residents in flat #20, and have seen around his quarters, which are quite salubrious.

Aaron said 'It's not that number', so I took it that he meant one of the other flats in the same block. Back in All Hallows I discussed this with the others and despite some mismatch between Aaron's description and what we actually knew of local accommodations, it looked likely that I would shortly be a close neighbour of Clarky and his frequently-to-be-found-there young acolyte, Ging.

The day of inspection visit arrived, my things were packed for the outcome; probably good; bad, although now unlikely, still possible. I counted down the last minutes to 10:40 the appointed time then I exited #24 and headed towards the Clarky.

I had anticipated that I would be hanging around outside for some ten minutes or so before Aaron's arrival-with-excuse, since on previous contacts he seemed to be one for whom appointed times represent an ambition rather than a firm commitment.

It just shows how wrong you can be; there he was on the opposite side of the road, hand aloft in greeting. And walking towards me was the first clue that the res I had imagined was not what was about to be offered.

Number 51, which is where I am now and may remain for a year or two, is almost opposite #24, the crazy house. It's actually about 3 doors further down the hill towards the school, but even girls could throw a stone from one address to the other.

Outside, the appearance is nothing special, there is an alley next to this property and such space attracts mischief, dog shit and fly-tipping. Not pretty. But there was an absence of dead fridges, bent bicycle wheels and dismantled chipboard furniture such as decorate the environs of many houses in this neighbourhood. Estate agents would have justification in calling the present degree of orderliness a 'feature' around here.

Next door, the lady occupant has an exuberant collection of flowers-in-pots in her front yard. I have yet to count them, but the number must be around thirty. She takes pride in how her house looks, few others do. The area to the front of #51 is empty apart from a set of recycling boxes and a starter collection of weeds. It wouldn't take much to brighten up; I'll get to that before long.

I haven't kept you in suspense for drama purpose, but on the day, as Aaron unlocked and I got the first glimpse of the interior of this place, it would be a reasonable use of the word to say that the contrast between outside and in was 'dramatic'.

I was about to step in to a new, I'll make that more prominent, **NEW**, new, new, new, new, new, new, new, new, new, new, new, new, new, new, new, flat.

It looked new; it smelled ditto, all the paint was new, the dark wood laminate flooring, well-underpadded carpet too. In the kitchen and bathroom fittings and decor were brand new. Have you ever been to new housing estate and looked around the show suite? That's what this place is like – no sign of use, apparently un-lived in.

Although the structure is the same age as the surrounding houses, the interior has been given a thorough refurbishment. I am a harsh critic of most modern building work, so am surprised and delighted by the quality of the renovations; the reno has been done to a high standard.

It's bloody incredible, ten days ago I was being dumped in an addicts' shooting gallery and today I'm being offered a show flat. This is another moment with a bit much to take in.

I bubble enthusiasm as we look around, then Aaron drives me back to the housing assoc's office for the formal hand-over ceremony, a dozen pages signed and that's it.

If this is all a dream, please leave me sleeping, I never want to wake up.

* * *

What has being homeless taught me?
The first thing to say is that I have nowhere found a straightforward guide to escaping homelessness.

This is surprising seeing as homelessness is a huge and expensive problem for society. Some aspects of the help that is available are described in sections of various websites, flyers and booklets – but a comprehensive guide, written in simple Plain English appears not to exist.

My account isn't the Dummy's Guide to Escaping Homelessness, but I do hope it gives insight into a number of the issues that you will face if you are of No Fixed Address. The tips about dealing with the authorities were hard won for me – I suggest close reading of them if you enter this netherworld.

* * *

The next point, and one which may have to be experienced before a person can grasp how determinant it is, when you are homeless, your ability to do anything constructive is reduced to a minimum; you are constantly focused on getting through the current day and dealing with all the immediate existential problems

If this difficulty is compounded by the debilitating effects of alcohol or drugs, there is really little chance of a person ever getting back to normal/conventional life.

There are many agencies which advertise that they offer help; my experience of them is mixed – often when I made contact, instead of engagement I was quickly referred to the next organisation down the line.

Latterly I have been helped by a couple of agencies which thus far seem to be competent, but that was after a number of disappointing experiences.

* * *

A surprise for me was that being homeless has put me in contact with many decent people. Much of my earlier career was spent with assertive, ambitious individuals often pretentious too. These traits are largely absent amongst those without fixed dwelling; I am in no hurry to return to the former crowd.

When you don't have the security, which many suppose leading a conventional life gives you, an alternative form of support manifests. At least it does if you let it - some unfortunate people don't or rather, can't. Time and again I have been surprised at how many people have been kind.

The organisations whose purpose is to offer help are less consistent - there are reasons for that. But amongst the individuals I meet, overwhelmingly they are friendly and concerned to do what they can.

* * *

I've touched on this before, but never given it the emphasis that it deserves; you don't need much money to live well.

The principles which have become clear to me over the last year are: think twice and thrice if you really need something. Probably you don't, but if it is absolutely necessary, see if you can borrow the item.

Myself I find that in most cases I can improvise. With a few basic tools, sewing, joinery, electrics many things are fixable.

In the UK we have excellent resources for the thrifty; charity shops, websites offering free goods, eBay, libraries, food banks, Poundland and similar stores. There is very little that a person needs to feed him/herself and survive which can't be bought for a pound an item.

My son Charlie in his first university year lived on a minimum (he didn't tell me until after), he said his eating was comprised principally of rice and ketchup (it would strain credulity if there wasn't an occasional döner kebab). I'm not telling you that you must restrict yourself to this degree, but on the other hand, there is little justification in dining in restaurants at £15 a head - or a multiple of that.

Quite how she achieved it I never got to know, but Julie, a colleague when I worked in the Netherlands told me that she could feed her family of four on ten Euros a week. A vegetarian diet must be a major part of this I imagine.

Owning a car is probably a needless expense. (Depends where you live of course.) My last one cost, all in, at least £1,000 a year to run. I sold it and since have mostly travelled by rideshare if taking a bus isn't adequate. On one occasion it was unavoidable to take a €30 taxi ride. Total costs for the year, no more than £200.

Cars sit parked for 90 per cent of their lives and are constant sources of expense. If you live in a place where the public transport is good enough, when you must have a car, hire one.

* * *

Our society has an addiction to stuff, things, purchasables, and it gets in the way of being a proper human. You don't need lots of things; what I have in one medium size suitcase and a backpack has been sufficient for almost a year. There's a full 20 foot shipping container of my other belongings in a distant location; I don't miss any of it much.

These are not original thoughts, wise men have taught the same throughout the ages; so why don't most of us live simply? Because commerce, the profit motive, read - greed, have deliberately, selfishly, abusively, blinded us to the obvious.

Our sources of information, those channels which offer us a particular model for existence, are controlled by just a few, need I say it, enormously wealthy individuals who are not driven to use their influence to achieve a world which is fairer and more enjoyable for all humanity. Instead what they crave and strive for is even greater wealth and a world according to their ideas.

If you own a chain of television stations and hence control what they broadcast, you form the thinking of millions. Since the revenue obtained from broadcasting comes from advertisers, inevitability you aim to please those clients.

Advertisers want to sell product and so we poor saps are on the receiving end of seductive messages crafted with the prostituted talent of creative people.

This could be a beautiful world where all make the most of their born abilities and have joyful lives. But it isn't; a few have more than they know what to do with and a multitude are trapped in deprivation, wasting their talents and potential.

The idea that owning lots and being rich makes you 'better' or happier is false. The richest people are those who feel good about their lives and that derives principally from having good family and social contacts and feeling that your work and existence are worthwhile.

The sentiment is captured in the following lines. I have lost the source, and I'm paraphrasing, sorry.

> *The rich man alone in his penthouse*
> *with his gadgets. The poor man in the*
> *pub having a laugh with his mates.*

This isn't just Robert playing guru; the World Happiness Report tells anyone who will listen exactly this message every year. Find it on line, read it and give it a good hard think.

* * *

I hope you have enjoyed my book, if you have questions or comments you can reach me at the address you'll find on the next page.

I'm heading out to The Crown Tavern for a pint now.

Have a nice life.

Robert

Thanks for reading this book!

I'd be very grateful if you'd post a short review on Amazon. Your support really does make a difference and I read all the reviews personally so I can get your feedback and make this book even better.

I have another book of my adventures in the works - if you would like a free review copy, just email me saying so and you'll be one of the first to read it.

robert@seviourbooks.com

Printed in Great Britain
by Amazon